A **Guide** to
Plymouth's Historic
Old Burial Hill

with

Stories from Behind the Grave Stones

Shipwrecks, Curses,
Intriguing Epitaphs,
Tragedies, Forgotten Wars,
Pilgrim Love Stories,
Puritan History
Includes:
Names Index with
Grave Location Indicator

By: Theodore P. Burbank

i

Published in the United States
By Salty Pilgrim Press
a division of
Parker-Nelson Publishing

Copyright ©2006 by Theodore P. Burbank.

www.SaltyPilgrim.com

ISBN 09645237-9-5

Salty Pilgrim Press
17 Causeway Street
Millis, MA 02054
508 794-1200

Preface

The engravings upon the gravestones found in New England's earliest cemeteries can be quite intriguing. Some gravestones provide faint clues into major or horrendous events. Others provide a glimpse into the person themselves. Some are humorous while others are sad or meant to provide a lesson. We have assembled a collection of such headstones and the stories behind the clues chiseled into the stones for eternity from Plymouth's Old Burial Hill Cemetery.

Below is an example of a gravestone that hints to an event in America's history. Can you determine to what event this gravestone may be a clue?

GRAVE OF BRITISH SOLDIERS

They came three thousand miles and died
to keep the past upon its throne
unheard beyond the ocean tide
Their English Mother made her moan
April 19 1775

Clues: British Soldiers, April 19, 1775, hmmm – the stone is found in Concord, Massachusetts

Answer: The "shot heard round the world" and the start of the American Revolution and the Battle at Lexington and Concord.

Introduction

This book is meant to be a guide through one of the oldest and most historic cemeteries in the United States of America. Clues into our history and evolution into the country we are today can be gleaned from the gravestones found high upon Old Burial Hill overlooking Plymouth Harbor, the Mayflower and Plymouth Rock.

It is ironic that the cemetery in the town that has memorialized the "First Comers" with streets, schools, businesses, shoals, streams and more all bearing their names does not have a single gravestone that marks a Mayflower passenger's grave contemporaneous with their death. Yes, the pilgrims buried their dead in unmarked graves!

There are several good reasons for this:
- Initially did not want the native Indians to know how weak their numbers were
- No stone carvers came aboard the Mayflower or other ships for some time
- No suitable stone source existed from which to fashion suitable headstones
- Headstones had to be imported from England at great expense
- The Pilgrims were much to occupied with surviving in the New World to devout much time, effort or treasure to carving headstones

The only headstone erected contemporaneous with the death of a Mayflower passenger can be found in Salem, Massachusetts. It marks the resting place of Richard More who died 1692 at 79 years of age. He was six when he landed in Plymouth.

Dedication

This book is dedicated to my father who would have been surprised and pleased to discover he was descended from six passengers aboard the Mayflower when it landed at Plymouth Rock in 1620.

While researching this book I was able to document and trace our family's roots back to; Myles Standish, William and Alice Mullens, Priscilla (Mullens) and John Alden plus George Soule.

Table of Contents

Page Number

The Oldest Gravestones on Burial Hill 1
Edward Gray, 1681 1
William Crowe 1683/84 2
Thomas Cushman 1691 3
Cushman Monument 3
Thomas Clark 1697 4
Hanna Clark 1697 5
John Cotton Jr., Rev 1640-1699 6
Dueling Pilgrims 7
Captain Nathaniel Carver 8
Dr William Thomas 9
Dr James Thatcher 10
Caleb Cooh 11
Capt. Benjamin Warren 12
Rev. Adoniram Judson 14
Mrs. Jane Dogget 15
Cross Dressing Patriots 17
General James Warren 19
General Nathaniel Goodwin 21
America's first foreign war casualty 23
Judge Thomas Russell 25
Captains Howard 26
Captain Gideon White 27
Captain Thomas Atwood and Mehitabel Atwood 28
Captain Atwood's children 29
Benjamin Harlow 29
Captain Abraham Hammatt 30
Thomas Faunce 31
Consider Howland 32
Causes of Death 33
Gravestone of a Child Bride? 36
Gravestone with an Attitude 37
Nameless Nobelman 38
A Double Whammy Curse 39
Another Cursed Howland 40
Pilgrim Murder 41

Puritan Thrift?	41
Madam Priscilla Hobart – A Puritan Love Story	42
Rev. James Kendall	45
Major William Bradford	49
The wreck of the General Arnold	50
Civil War Brother Casualties	53
Nathaniel Morton	54
Forefather's Monument	55
Holocaust in Ireland	57
Irish Freedom Fighter and Holocaust Survivor in Exile?	58
Early Gravestone Carvers	59
Alexander Scammell	60
America's First Naval Battle Fought Without a Navy	61
Thomas W Hayden	62
Lieutenant Frederick Holmes	63
US Presidents with Mayflower Heritage	65
First Ladies and Vice Presidents with Mayflower Heritage	67
Mayflower Royalty and Pilgrim Bigamist	68
Governor William Bradford	72
Early Pastors and Elders of the First Church	73
The Fortune – 1621	74
The ships *Anne* and *Little James* – 1623	75
Civil War Veterans on Burial Hill	77
War of 1812 Veterans on Burial Hill	78
Revolutionary War Veterans on Burial Hill	78
Mayflower Compact 1620	79
Mayflower Passengers	80
Familiar Names with Mayflower Roots	84
John Clarke	85
Smallpox	86
William Drew Tufts	87
Joseph Churchill	88
Stone Tops	89
Coll. Isaac Lothrop	91
William Ring	92
Joseph Bartlett	93
Revd. Chandler Robbins, DD	94
Pilgrim Promoter A. S. Burbank	95
Index of Names and Grave Location	97 thru 126
Sources	127

The Oldest Gravestones on Burial Hill

Six Seventeenth Century Stones

Edward Gray, 1681- Section I
William Crowe, 1683/84 - Section G
Thomas Cushman, 1691 - Section O
Thomas Clark, 1697 - Section K
Hannah Clark, 1697 - Section K
John Cotton Jr., Reverend, 1640-1699 - Section J

Edward Gray, 1681.

His gravestone is the oldest marker on Burial Hill in Plymouth. He came to Plymouth with a brother Thomas in 1643, at the age of fourteen years. Thomas died eleven years later in 1654. The boys reportedly were smuggled out of England by relatives who wanted the boy's inheritance. Edward was reportedly a descendant of Henry I King of France.

Edward became a merchant doing business on Main Street between Leyden and Middle streets. In 1651 he married Mary, daughter of John Winslow (brother of Gov. Edward Winslow). In 1665 Edward Gray married Dorothy Lettis who owned lands, also on Main street in Plymouth, giving Gray control over both sides of Main street. He was said to be the wealthiest man in Plymouth colony. He also was deputy to the general court from Plymouth from 1679 and 1680.

1

William Crowe, 1683/84. The stone of
William Crowe, the next in order of date, is of purple slate typical of headstones imported from England and is inscribed: --

Here lies buried
ye body of Mr
William Crowe
Aged About 55 years
who decd January
1683/4

William Crow immigrated to Plymouth from Ireland in order to escape the religious and political upheaval of the time. Said to have been a merchant in Plymouth. He married Hannah Winslow April 1, 1664. Hannah was the daughter of Josiah Winslow (brother of Gov. Edward Winslow)

---

n 1970 it was discovered that
Richard More and his siblings were not mere waifs on the *Mayflower*, as had been supposed, but were instead royally descended.

Thomas Cushman, 1691.

Thomas Cushman arrived at Plymouth Colony with his father Robert on the "Fortune" in 1621 and settled in that part of Plymouth that is now Kingston.

He was brought up and educated in the family of Governor Bradford and in 1636 Thomas married Mary Allerton.

He was appointed successor to Elder Brewster as Ruling Elder of the Plymouth church in 1649, continuing in the office for forty three years until his death, Dec. 11, 1691. He was also Governor's assistant for several years and went to London five times to serve the interests of the Colony. The church erected his gravestone twenty-five years after his death.

Cushman Monument

The largest monument to be found on Old Burial Hill in Plymouth is the Cushman obelisk erected by their grateful ancestors on August 15th 1885 to honor their venerated ancestors; Robert Cushman, the right hand of the Plymouth forefathers, and Elder Thomas Cushman, his son.

3

Thomas Clark – 1697

His ancient stone reads, Mr. Thomas Clarke died Mar. 24, 1697, aged 98 years. Descendants erected a larger stone nearby in 1891.

Here lies buried ye
body of
Mr. Thomas Clarke,
aged 98.
Departed this life
March 24, 1697.

This stone is erected to his
memory by his descendants
A.D.1891.

Thomas Clarke came to Plymouth from England aboard the ship *Anne* 1623. He married Susan Ring of Plymouth, 1634. He married his second wife, Mrs. Alice Hallett Nichols of Boston, in 1664. He lived for some years in Boston, and also in Harwich, of which town he was one of the original proprietors. He died in Plymouth, having lived in the reigns of six British sovereigns.

Thomas volunteered for service in the Pequot War, and was the thirteenth person in Capt. Miles Standish's third company in 1627. During his life he aspired to be a lawyer. He lived for 98 years.

Thomas Clark, or Clarke, not to be confused with John Clarke "mate of the '*Mayflower.*'" Rather, it has been argued that this Thomas Clark was the son of John Clark of Ratliff, pilot of the *Mayflower.*

Hannah Clark – 1697

Mrs. Hannah CLARKE,
Wife to Mr. William
Clarke,
Died Feb. 20 1687,
In her 29th year

Hannah may be the second wife the William Clarke whose first wife Sarah and children were massacred by the King Philip Indians ten years earlier.

William and Sarah Clarke "lived in a garrison house by Eel river, which was surprised by the Indians on a Sunday, March 12, 1676, while he was at church. His wife, several of his children, and some other persons, eleven in all, were killed in this attack, which is said to have been the only serious one ever made on the settlement.

William Clarke's son Thomas was left for dead, but afterwards recovered, and had a silver plate put over his exposed brain, by the celebrated surgeon Dr. John Clarke, of Boston. He ever afterwards was known as 'Silver-headed Tom.'
—*Baylies' History.*"

John Cotton Jr., Reverend 1640-1699

His edition of John Eliot's Indian Language Bible was published in 1685

Most people are surprised to learn that the first Bible printed in America was not printed in English or any other European language. In fact, English and European language Bibles would not be printed in America for more than 100 years!

His father was the John Cotton who in 1633 served as "teacher" of the First Church of Boston after escaping the persecution of Nonconformists by the Church of England. Rev. Cotton Jr. was excommunicated from his father's church for "three aggravating offences". He made an open confession and was restored in one month.

John Jr. was graduated from Harvard in 1657, studied theology with the Rev. Samuel Stone of Hartford, Conn., and from 1659 to 1663 preached at Wethersfield, Conn. He was married at Wethersfield, Conn., Nov. 7, 1660, to Joanna, daughter of Dr. Bray, .and had eleven children. In 1664 he learned the Algonquin Indian tongue and preached to the Indians at Martha's Vineyard for two years. He was the third pastor of the first church of Plymouth serving from *1669–1697*.

He was dismissed by the church October 5, 1697 "under very unpleasant circumstances". In November 1698 he accepted a call to Charleston, S.C., where he contracted and died of yellow fever.

Dueling Pilgrims

Edward Doty and Edward Lester, of the
Massachusetts colony, fought the first recorded American
duel in 1621, just a year after the Pilgrims arrived at
Plymouth. Armed with swords, both men sustained minor
wounds. A unique aspect of this duel was that Doty and
Leicester were servants. For the most part, only
gentlemen dueled.

Edward Doty, who had traveled as a servant of Hopkins',
was convicted of dueling with Edward Leister (also one of
Hopkins' servants) and was sentenced to have his head
tied to his heels for one hour.

The duel was fought over Desire Minter who later
returned to England unwed.

In 1638 Arthur Peach, Thomas Jackson,
Richard Stinnings and Daniel Cross
were convicted of robbing and murdering
an Indian named Penowanyanquis.
Daniel Cross escaped custody,
but the others were executed by hanging.

Captain Nathaniel Carver

He Saved Britain's Admiral Horatio Nelson from Capture by the French

While an Ensign, Nathaniel Carver was stationed at Fort Andrew on the Gurnet to guard the entrance to Plymouth harbor. It was here where he engaged in his first battle. The British ship H.M.S. Niger and the fort exchanged cannon fire and the Niger eventually was driven off. There were no casualties except for the hole in one of the Gurnet's twin lighthouses caused by a cannon ball fired from the Niger.

Captured and Released by a Grateful Captor

Later as Captain, he commanded a vessel which was captured by Britain's famous Admiral Nelson. While in custody Captain Carver was able to do the great naval officer a good turn by serving as a pilot for Nelson in his escape from a French squadron. In return, and as evidence of his gratitude, Admiral Nelson gave Captain Carver back his ship and freed both he and his men from captivity as this document below testifies.

"These are to certify that I took the schooner Harmony, Nathaniel Carver, master, belonging to Plymouth, but on ace't of his good services have given him up his vessel again."
Dated on b'd Ifis Majesty's Ship Albemarle, 7 Aug., 1782, in Boston Bay. Horatio Nelson.
Source: Plymouth Hall Museum

Dr. William Thomas

In the Battle for Louisburg

On the west side of the hill is the grave of Dr. William Thomas, a surgeon in the expedition against Louisburg in 1745. The French had spent millions to develop fortifications at Louisburg on Cape Briton Island, Canada in order to gain strategic advantage in a possible invasion of New England.

The colonialists, lead by William Pepperrell, captured the fortifications at Louisburg in a stunningly successful raid. Boston's Louisburg Square was so named to commemorate this victory.

Dr. Thomas owned one of the four slaves, Prince Goodwin, to serve in the Revolutionary Army. Prince apparently deserted in 1777 after serving three months. In 1778 the other three slaves were granted their freedom. Because of his desertion Prince Goodwin was not awarded his.

Source: The Plymouth Colony Archive Project

Dr. James Thatcher

Did his pen cause the crack in Plymouth Rock?

Dr. James Thatcher, surgeon with the Continental Army from 1775 through 1781, was born in Barnstable, Massachusetts, in 1754 and is considered to be the principal historian of the Revolutionary War.

He served with the Army from Bunker Hill to Yorktown and wrote a full and interesting journal which is one of the most complete diaries of the war.

In 1832 he wrote "The History of the Town of Plymouth," the popularity of which had unfortunate and unintended consequences as people began taking pieces of Plymouth Rock as souvenirs. As a result on July 4, 1834 the Rock was moved and placed in an enclosure. It was during this move that Plymouth Rock acquired its famous crack by falling off of the wagon.

Caleb Cook

His gun ended the King Philip War

 Caleb Cook was a soldier in Captain Church's unit and was the person who shot and killed the warring Indian Chief "King Philip" at the battle of Mount Hope, Rhodes Island.

King Philip attacked 52 settlements from the Connecticut Valley to Cape Cod. Twelve towns, including Plymouth, were burned or totally destroyed.

After the initial raids in 1675, Philip's forces struck Brookfield, Mendon, Northfield, Deerfield, Hadley, Springfield, Longmeadow, Hatfield, Simsbury, Northampton, Sudbury, Groton, Medfield, Lancaster, Marlborough, Andover, Billerica, Chelmsford, Natick, Woburn, Haverhill, Braintree, Weymouth, Scituate, Warwick, Wickfield, Bridgewater, Rehoboth (again), Providence and Plymouth.

His body was quartered and the parts hung from trees. His decapitated head was brought to Plymouth and staked on a pole, where it remained on view for more than twenty-five years.

The excerpt on the next page provides graphic details of the fateful final encounter.

*"Captain Church, knowing of Philip's
timidity and believing that if an attack was
made upon his front Philip would be the
first to escape by the rear, posted an
Englishman (Caleb Cook) with Alderman in
ambush at the edge of the swamp and Philip
was killed in his attempt to escape in the
exact way in which Captain Church had
anticipated, i.e. he had "catched up his gun,
thrown his powder-horn over his head and
ran into the ambush with no more clothes
than his small breeches and stockings only
to fall on his face in the mud and water,
with his gun under him and a bullet
through his heart".*

King Philip

**President George W. Bush and
Sen. John Kerry are ninth cousins, twice removed,
and descended from William Bradford.**

12

Capt. Benjamin Warren

He married five wives, the last marriage taking place fifty-eight years after the first. He died in 1746 at 76 years of age

Paul Revere Engraved his Compass Roses

Colonel Benjamin Warren was a compass maker and silversmith Paul Revere did the engraving for the compass roses used in his surveying compasses.

There were five generations of Warrens in Plymouth, Massachusetts before 1800, all named Benjamin.

Colonel Benjamin Warren, the compass maker, died at Plymouth in 1825 and his grave is not to be found on Burial Hill..

Rev. ADONIRAM JUDSON,

Congregationalist Minister and Father of Baptist Missionaries

Many visitors to Burial Hill will search for the white marble slab which stands as a memorial to the Judson family.
Sacred to the memory of
Rev. ADONIRAM JUDSON,
who died NOV. 28, 1826, Æ. 75.
A faithful and devoted Minister of Christ.

Father of Baptist Missionaries

Adoniram Judson D. D. taught himself to read at the age of three, and by his tenth year he knew Latin and Greek and was a serious student of theology. At the age of 16 he entered Brown University and was graduated three years later as the valedictorian of his class. At Andover Theological Seminary he could not get away from the words "Go ye into all the world" and would spend his life as a missionary. He is often referred to as "the Father of Baptist Missionaries."

American Baptist missionary, lexicographer, and Bible translator to Burma. Born in Massachusetts in 1788. Helped form the American Baptist Missionary Union. In 1834 completed a translation of the whole Bible into the Burmese language. During the Anglo-Burmese War, he spent twenty-one months in prison.

14

From 1845-1847, after thirty-four years in Burma, he took his only furlough to his native land. Returning to Burma, he spent his remaining years working on his English-Burmese dictionary. He died in 1850 and was buried at sea.

Judson wrote two famous hymn-poems, "Our Father God, Who Art in Heaven" (1825) and "Come, Holy Spirit, Dove Divine" (1832). Judson Memorial Church in New York City is dedicated to his memory. He was married 3 times. His first wife is buried in Burma; his second at St Helena (off of Africa) and the 3rd (who raised his children) is buried in Hamilton NY at Madison Avenue Cemetery.

The voyage took 66 days to cross the Atlantic. The first child born in New England after the ship arrived was Peregrine White, son of William and Susanna White. The landing took place on November 11, 1620, at present day Provincetown, Mass., at the tip of Cape Cod.

Mrs Jane Dogget

A most graphic yet mysterious epitaph

To the memory of the amiable
Mrs. Jane. Dogget
Consort of Mr. Seth Dogget
who died May 31 1794
in the 26th year of her age
also an infant Daughter by
her side

*Come view the seen twill fill
you with surprise
Behold the loveliest form in
nature dies
At noon she flourish'd
blooming fair and gay
At evening an extended corpse
she lay.*

Mary, widow of Elder Cushman and Daughter
of Isaac Allerton, Died November 28, 1699
Aged about 83. She was the last survivor of
the first comers of the *Mayflower*.

Cross Dressing Patriots

Capt. Simeon Sampson

*O ye whose cheek the tear of
pity stains Draw near with pious
reverence and attend
Here lie the loving Husbands
dear remains The tender Father
and the courteous Friend
The dauntless heart yet
touched by human woe A Friend
to man to vice alone a Foe.*

Two Firsts

Captain Simeon Sampson was a naval hero during the
Revolutionary War. He was the first naval officer to be
commissioned by the Massachusetts Provincial Congress.
He commanded the 16 gun brigantine Independence, the first
warship built for the Revolutionary Provincial Government. The
Independence was built at the Drew shipyard at Kingston and
launched in July of 1776.

Capture, Cross Dressing and Escape

Captain Sampson was captured by the Royal Navy during
an engagement off Halifax, Nova Scotia. Although
officers were expected to surrender their swords upon
capture, Captain Sampson had his sword returned to him
by the British commander in recognition of Sampson's
courage and valor. Captain Sampson soon made his
escape from capture by the British by disguising himself
in woman's clothing.

He would later command the Kingston-built ships *Hazard* and *Mars*. His sword can be viewed today in Pilgrim Hall Museum in Plymouth and his stone found on the northerly side of the Old Burial Hill near the path leading from School to Russell Streets.

Famous Niece - *America's First Woman Warrior*

Capt. Sampson's niece, Deborah Sampson (b. 17 Dec 1760 d. 29 Apr 1827) was the first known American woman to impersonate a man in order to join the army and take part in combat. At the age of nineteen, she disguised herself as a boy and took the name "Timothy Thayer" as her alias.

She was wounded several times and, in order to conceal her true gender, she cared for the first few by herself. However, wounds sustained during battle in Pennsylvania were severe enough to require the attention of a physician. The doctor kept her secret and she was released from service to heal.

Word of her duplicity apparently leaked out as later she was excommunicated from the First Baptist Church of Middleborough, Massachusetts, because of a strong suspicion that she was "dressing in man's clothes and enlisting as a Soldier in the Army."

Gen. James Warren

Did his Brother in Law start the American Revolution?

 General James Warren, a lineal descendant of Mayflower passenger Richard Warren, graduated Harvard in 1745. He was Plymouth County Sheriff and held the positions of Paymaster General and chief commissary officer of the Revolutionary Army in Massachusetts. General Warren was elected to the Legislature and was Speaker of the Massachusetts House for two years.

During his tenure in the Massachusetts legislator the Constitution of the United States was ratified. His wife was Mercy Otis Warren and together they had five children. She was a distinguished person in her time and was noted for her powerful mind and was active in the politics of the day. Mercy wrote several plays which stirred colonial patriotism including "The Sack of Rome" and "The Ladies of Castile."

"No taxation without representation" and "Every man's home is his castle" were the phrases, uttered during a fiery speech given by James Otis II. No Taxation Without Representation eventually would become the rallying cry of the American Revolution. John Adams said of the speech, "the American nation was born in that moment." James Otis II was Mercy Otis Warren's brother.

Born in 1725 in Barnstable, he received his MA degree from Harvard in 1743, and was King's Advocate General of the Vice Admiralty Court and successful lawyer. The British issued the "Writs of Assistance" in 1775 which were essentially search warrants that did not name the place to be searched and were issued in perpetuity. Otis considered the writs a nothing more than a license to steal. He resigned his post, in part as revenge for being passed over for the post of Chief Justice of the Massachusetts Superior Court, and took up the defense of the colonists.

U-S-History.com:

In 1769, at the height of his popularity and influence, Otis was pulled from the public stage. He had infuriated a Boston custom-house official with a vicious newspaper attack; the official beat Otis on his head with a cane. For the remainder of his life, Otis was subject to long bouts of mental instability. He was unable to participate in public affairs and spent most of his time wandering through the streets of Boston.

He endured the taunts of a populace that had quickly forgotten his contributions. Otis was struck by lightning and died in May 1783.

John Billington's sons John and Francis nearly blew up the Mayflower while the ship was sitting in Provincetown Harbor when they shot off a gun near an open barrel of gunpowder.

General Nathaniel Goodwin

The Yankee Doodle Patriot

In Memory of

Gen. Nathaniel Goodwin,

*Who departed this life
Mar. 8, 1819,
aged 70 years*

Reportedly he was the "Cap'n Gooding" referred to in the third verse of the song "Yankee Doodle."

*Yankee Doodle went to town
A-riding on a pony
Stuck a feather in his hat
And called it macaroni.*

*Yankee Doodle, keep it up
Yankee Doodle dandy
Mind the music and the step
And with the girls be handy.*

*Father and I went down to camp
Along with **Captain Gooding**
And there we saw the men and boys
As thick as hasty pudding.*

*Yankee Doodle, keep it up
Yankee Doodle dandy
Mind the music and the step
And with the girls be handy*

*There was Captain Washington
Upon a slapping stallion
A-giving orders to his men
I guess there was a million.*

*Yankee Doodle, keep it up
Yankee Doodle dandy
Mind the music and the stepAnd
with the girls be handy.*

General Goodwin was in charge of enlistments for the Revolutionary army in the Plymouth County. The Pilgrim Society has Goodwin's (then a Lieutenant Colonel) very detailed recruiting and enlistment records for the years 1776 to 1781 in Pilgrim Hall.

In addition to the soldier's name and residence Goodwin's records also record the persons: age, stature, complexion, eye and hair color, trade, and the term and date of enlistment. 42 men identified by the terms "Negro," "Black," or "Mulatto," and 20 are identified as being "Indians."

His house once stood where the Baptist church now stands.

In 1648, Alice Bishop was convicted of murder by slashing her sleeping four year old daughter Martha's throat. She was hung by the neck until dead.

"...to the shores of Tripoli"

He was one of America's First Casualty
of a Foreign War

Dr. John GODDARD,
surgeon of the U.S. frigate
Boston, died in Gibraltar Bay
June 18, 1802, aged 32 years.
Also Grace Hyman, his wife, died
Feb. 8, 1851, aged 80 years. And
of Abigail Otis, died Feb. 11,
1853 in her 70th year

The First Barbary War, (1801-1805) also known as the Barbary Coast War or the Tripolitan War, was fought against Ottoman Empire run piratical military strongmen who were financed by ransom, plunder, and tribute. It was America's first war abroad or foreign war.

At the end of the Revolution, America became solely responsible for the safety of its own commerce and citizens. No longer was American shipping in the Mediterranean protected by the English Navy. Without the means or the authority to field a naval force the budding U.S. government took a more pragmatic but ultimately self-destructive route and allocated money for payment of tribute to the pirates for protection of its commerce and seamen.

The U.S. paid up to $1 million per year over 15 years for the safe passage of American ships and/or the return of American hostages. Payments in ransom and tribute to the privateering states amounted to 20 percent of United States government annual revenues in 1800.

On Jefferson's inauguration as president in 1801 the pasha of Tripoli demanded a tribute of $225,000 from the new administration. Jefferson refused the demand and consequently the pasha declared war on the United States.

Jefferson sent a group of frigates, including the US frigate *Boston*, to defend American interests in the Mediterranean in response. In 1802, the 28-gun US frigate Boston fought an action with six or seven Tripolitanian gunboats, forcing one ashore.

The First Barbary War proved that America could execute a war far from home, and that American forces had the cohesion to fight together as Americans and not just as Virginians or New Yorkers. This war is memorialized in the Marine Hymn; *"to the shores of Tripoli."*

US frigate *Boston*

America's first guided missile ship is named after Dr. Goddard's US frigate *Boston*.

USS *Boston* (CAG-1)

Judge Thomas Russell

Abolitionists Activist and Supporter of James Brown

Judge Thomas Russell and his wife Mary Ellen were Abolitionists. The Russell's were good friends with James Brown, a Connecticut-born abolitionist and the leader of the infamous raid on Harper's Ferry. In addition to the Harper's Ferry raid Brown and six companions dragged five proslavery men and boys from their beds at Pottawatomie Creek, Kansas, split open their skulls, cut off their hands, and laid out their entrails.

A war of revenge erupted in Kansas. Columns of proslavery Southerners ransacked free farms while they searched for Brown. At Osawatomie, proslavery forces attacked Brown's headquarters, leaving a dozen men dead. Before it was over, guerrilla warfare in Kansas left 200 dead.

The Judge and his wife traveled all the way to Charlestown, Virginia from Boston to attend their friend's trial reportedly to determine the truth of the tales of atrocities allegedly committed by Brown and his followers. Standing in the shadows of the gallows that soon would send him into eternity Brown disavowed having anything to do with the killings. John Brown was hanged on December 2, 1859.

Thomas Russell was president of the Pilgrim Society and took as active interest in the history of the town of Plymouth

Captains Howard

Captains Lost at Sea

Capt James Howard

Died June 15, 1818
At St. Martins, West
Indies
aged 41 years

In memory of John W.
Howard Son of Capt.
James Howard & Mrs.
Hannah his wife
born March 20, 1815
died April 2, 1815

He glanc'd into the world
to see
A sample of our misery.

Captain Gideon White, *Loyalist*

Left his family in Plymouth and died in exile

 Captain Gideon White, one of the original members of Old Colony Club founded in 1769 and known today as the "Pilgrim Society", is not buried on Old Burial Hill but his wife and children are. It is assumed that he along with many Loyalists of the time went to Nova Scotia and settled there.

Between 1765 and 1775, the Allegiance and self-identity of the American colonists changed dramatically. In this ten year period of time, many previously loyal English citizens became armed rebels refusing to acknowledge the sovereignty of the crown.

Choices were not clear or easy during these turbulent years as armed conflict with England became increasingly apparent. Families and communities were torn apart as the division of those wishing to remain loyal to the king, Loyalists, and those who desired freedom or Revolutionaries, formed and solidified.

There was no school in the early years of New Plymouth. Parents taught their children to learn to read and write themselves or with help of neighbors.

27

Capt Thomas Atwood and Mehitabel Atwood

He was a direct descendant of John Alden and was born in 1768 and died on 14 Jan 1808. His wife, Mehitabel, died exactly a year from the day of her beloved husband's passing. Her epitaph graphically describes the toll of loosing three children and a husband in short order takes.

Erected to the memory, of Mrs. MEHITABEL, wife of Capt. Thos. Atwood, who died Jan, 11, 1809,

In the 38 year of her age. In early life her feeble constitution gave painful premonition of her early exit.
She however unexpectedly passed the meridian of life, discharging in a very laudable manner, filial parental & conjugal duties.
At length the seeds of death were planted in her vitals --
she sickened, languished & expired in hopes of a blessed immortality.

Short is our longest day of life,
And soon its prospect ends
Yet on that day's uncertain date
Eternity depends.

Captain Atwood's Children

Twin daughters of
Capt. Atwood
and Mehetabel his wife

born Nov. 2, 1802
died Nov. 4, 1802
Also
Darius, son of Capt Thomas and
Mehetabel his wife

died Jan 23, 1809 ,
Aged 2 months & 8 days

Darius died 12 days after his father's passing

Benjamin Harlow

In memory of
Mr. Benjamin Harlow
who died November 18th 1816
aged 34 years.

*Friends and physicians could not
save
My mortal Body from the Grave
Nor can the Grave confine me
here
When Christ the son of God
appears*

29

Captain Abraham Hammatt - 1797

The "Shot heard 'round the world" might have been fired from Marshfield

In This sacred spot
Are deposited the remains of
Capt. Abraham Hammatt
who died of a malignant Fever
October 12th 1797 Ætatis 47
And of his daughter Sophia who
On the fst December following
Fell a victim to the same
Disease Ætatis 13.

*Hers was the mildness of the
rising Morn
And his the radiance of the
risen day.*

At the time of the battle of Lexington and Concord, April 19, 1775, where the "shot heard around the world" was fired, a company of British troops called the "Queen's Guards," was stationed at Marshfield. Upon receiving word of the battle at Concord and Lexington they left Marshfield on April 20th and withdrew back to Boston.

That same day Captain Abraham Hammatt's company of Minute-men, under command of Col. Theophilus Cotton began their march from Plymouth to Marshfield to confront the Queen's Guard. When the company arrived in Marshfield the British were gone. Marshfield could well have been the scene of the first bloodshed in the Revolutionary War had the battles at Concord and Lexington not occurred the day before.

Thomas Faunce

Did he save Plymouth Rock from destruction?

Here lyes buried the Body
of
Mr. THOMAS Faunce
ruling
Elder of the first Church
of Christ in
Plymouth deceased Febry
27th An : Dom. 1745/6
in the 99th year of his
Age.

The Fathers,
where are they?
Blessed are the dead who
Die in the Lord.

No mention of Plymouth Rock can be found in any of the Mayflower passenger's writings. In fact no mention can be found for more than one hundred years after the Pilgrims landing in Plymouth. The rock was apparently not of much importance in the early years as the Pilgrims were engaged in more pressing survival matters.

In 1741 plans were afoot for the construction of a wharf at the bottom of Cole's Hill. Thomas Faunce, Elder of the church and then in his nineties, objected that the wharf would cover the exact rock his father, who arrived aboard the *Anne* in 1623, had pointed out to him as the landing spot upon which the Pilgrims first set foot in Plymouth. As Plymouth Rock might be damaged or destroyed during construction of the wharf, plans were changed and Plymouth Rock was saved for posterity because of Elder Thomas Faunce.

Consider Howland.

Captured and traded for his Loyalist cousin

Consider Howland,
born 1745,
died October 1780,
lost at sea, age 35.

He is memorialized on
his brother Thomas'
tombstone

Consider Howland was aboard the ship *Washington* when
it was captured off Plymouth by the British Man-o-War
HMS Foley on December 2, 1775. He along was among
the 74 shipped to England as prisoners of war. By
February of 1776 only 21 remained alive due to an
outbreak of smallpox.

In September of 1777, Howland was exchanged for his
own first cousin - Captain Gideon White, a Loyalist from
Plymouth, captured while sailing on a ship provisioning
the British army. Howland returned to sea, first as
master of the privateer *Nancy*, then as first lieutenant of
the sloop *America,* a privateer fitted out in Plymouth.

In July of 1880, he was given command of the
privateering schooner *Phoenix.* Consider never returned
from that voyage

Causes of Death

Many stones reference the cause of death:

By Lightening

BATHSHEBA JAMES
widow of Capt William Holmes 3d
Mariner and daughter to Capt
Joseph Doten Do.
:he was killed instantaneously in a
under storm by the Electrich fluid
lightning on the 6th of July 1830,
aged 35 years and 26 days.
She was an affectionate wife; a
utiful Daughter, a happy mother, a
kind and sincere friend.

*1s sweet Blossom short was the period that
thy enlivening virtues contributed to the
Happiness of those connections;
ut oh, how long have they to moum the loss
of so much worth and Excellence.*

By Lightening and Lost at Sea

This stone chronicles a seafaring family's tragedies

GEORGE STRAFFIN
Died Jan. 10, 1801, aged 32
years
Killed by lightening
in the Bay of Biscay.
Mary Widow of above died Mar.
30, 1843, aged 73 years.
Two sons, George died at sea
July7, 1824 in his 26th year
Robert Lost at sea,
Jan 1821 aged 21 years

Straight to the point

Beza Hayward Jr.

Son of

Beza Hayward Esq.

Who was Drowned in
Plymouth Harbor

Feb 5, 1814
in his 22nd year

More detail

Father Mother
To the memory of
Capt. GEORGE BACON
Who was drowned at sea on a
voyage from Hamburg
to New York
Sept. 6, 1826 AE 53 yrs
ELIZABETH
His widow died
Jan. 6, 1859
Aged 79 yrs & 4 months

There is rest in heaven

34

A short and not so sweet story

James Jordan.

Drowned in Smelt Pond, June 25, 1837, aged 27 y'rs.

Buried on the day he was to have been married.

Gravestone with a Disclaimer

This inscription is not to be found on Old Burial Hill but rather on a gravestone in Vine Hill Cemetery, Plymouth. It tells another kind of story and even contains a disclaimer and we thought it worthy of inclusion here.

JOHN T. McMAHON
1930 -
HE WAS A FAILURE AS A HUSBAND AND FATHER
HE WAS INSANE 15 YEARS BECAUSE OF LIQUOR
BUT DIED SOBER
MAY CHRIST HAVE MERCY ON HIS SOUL
HE WAS NOT A PILGRIM

The Pilgrims were summoned to church services by the beating of a drum.

Gravestone of a Child Bride?

This stone found in Plymouth's Old Burial Hill near the
Russell Street parking lot, apparently got past the
teacher, the editor and the elders as well. Was Captain
Brews' wife actually only four years old when she
perished?

Capt Ellis Brews
and Mrs. Nancy
wife died Dec 13 180
aged 4 years

Actually this is a broken stone that probably refers to Captain Ellis
Brewster as the inscriptions on a stone found at Plymouth's Oak
Grove & Vine Hills Cemetery in the CHURCHILL-BREWSTER-
BRAMHALL Plot indicates.

NANCY
Widow of DANIEL CHURCHILL
Born Jan'y 1, 1769
Died Oct 8, 1857
Also her first husband
Ellis Brewster
who died at Sea Aug 27, 1817
in the 49 year of his age.
Also their son
WILLIAM E. BREWSTER
Died Dec 13, 1809
Aged 4 years.

Gravestone with an Attitude

The epitaph on this stone in Plymouth's Old Burial Hill certainly reflects an attitude.

In memory of
Mrs. Tabitha Plasket
who died June 10, 1807
Aged 64 years.

*Adieu vain world I have seen
enough of thee
and I am careless what thou
sayst of me
Thy smiles I wish not Nor thy
frowns I fear
I am now at rest my head lies
quiet here*

It turns out that Tabitha Plasket was for many years a school-teacher in Plymouth and was well known as an eccentric character. She is also referred to as America's first schoolteacher according to a biography in Daughters of the America Revolution Magazine.

Plymouth Colony only had two witch trials
during its history, and in both cases
the accuser was found guilty
of libel and punished.

37

The "Nameless Nobleman"

The hero of Mrs. Jane G. Austin's historical novel of that title published in 1881 was extremely popular with forty printings, the last being in 1909, was reportedly based upon the life of the Dr. Le Barran buried on Plymouth's Old Burial Hill.

Here lyes ye body of

Mr. FRANCIS LE BARRAN

phytician who
departed this life
Augst ye 18th 1704,
in ye 36 year
of his age.

Le Barran was the surgeon aboard a French ship which shipwrecked in Buzzards Bay in 1694. Officers and crew were taken prisoner and, while on their way to Boston for Imprisonment, stopped in Plymouth for the night. When it became known Le Barron was a surgeon it was requested that he perform an operation which he did successfully. The people of Plymouth requested the lieutenant governor allow Le Barran to stay in town. The request was granted for which the many Le Barons descendants in America are grateful

A Double Whammy Curse?

The historical novel "Dr. Le Baron and His Daughters" by Jane G. Austin tells of a young sailor named Ansel Ring who was cursed by an old witch referred to as Mother Crewe. Ansel lies with his shipmates who perished on board the "General Arnold" Christmas Day 1778. Was witch Crewe's curse responsible for the tragic wreck that took the lives of so many sailors?

Hannah Howland is said to have died of a broken heart on account of her lover Ansel Ring's tragic demise. Her stone on the top of Old Burial Hill reads:

Sic Traneit Gloria Mundi
To the memory of Miss
Hannah Howland,
who died of a
Languishment,
January ye 25th 1780
Ætatis 26.
For us they languish, &
for us they die
And shall they languish
shall they die in vain

Was the curse of the old witch Mother Crewe responsible for these deaths? There are many who would say yes. People of Plymouth considered Mother Crewe to be evil and generally gave her a wide berth. She was accused of driving ships ashore, blighting land, accepting money to infecting a young woman with small pox among other things.

The John Billington family
was the only family that
did not lose a family member
that terrible first winter in Plymouth.

Another Cursed Howland

Southward Howland demanded Dame Crewe's house and land, claiming under law of entail (ownership is restricted through inheritance to biological descendants) and primogeniture (inheritance by only the eldest son). Howland was arrogant and the woman's house was in a good location, so he rode to her door and claimed possession of the house and land demanding she be gone before he tore the house down on Friday next.

Mother Crewe's reply was "On Friday they'll dig your grave on Burying Hill. I see the shadow closing round you. You draw it in with every breath. Quick! Home and make your peace!"

Howland's reply, "Bandy no witch words with me, woman. On Friday I will return." And he swung himself into his saddle. As he did so a black cat sitting upon Mother Crewe's shoulder sprang onto the horse's rump clawing and hissing, sending the frightened horse off at an uncontrollable gallop.

In a high pitched shrill voice she shouted after him, "My curse is on you here and hereafter. Die! Then go down to hell!" An eerie fog descended over the town and a chill filled the air. Before darkness had fallen the dead body of Southward Howland was found laying on the ground. His corpse was buried on Friday in the Old Burial Hill Cemetery.

Pilgrim Murder

John Billington who, after a few legal run-ins, was found guilty in 1630 of murdering John Newcomen. He was hanged. William Bradford, as governor, recorded what happened in his journal.

"John Billington the elder, one that came over with the first, was found guilty of willful murder by plain and notorious evidence. And was accordingly executed. He and some of his had often been punished before, being one of the profanest families among them; they came from London. He waylaid a young man, one John Newcomen, about a former quarrel and shot him with a gun, whereof he died."

Puritan Thrift?

Ten names on one modest stone

Samuel H
Josiah ye
n John Cotton
Josiah Anonymus Edward
Josiah Edward Richard Roland
7 sons of Josiah Cotton
who died between
ye year 1712 & 1734

Madam Priscilla Hobart

A Puritan Love Story

Departed this Life
June 23, 1796,
In the 90th year of her Age
Madam Priscilla Hobart
Relict
of the Revd Noah Hobart
late of Fairfield in Connecticut
her third husband
her first and Second
were
John Watson Esq and
Honble Isaac Lothrop.

The following was written by Rev. John L. Watson, D.D., of Orange, N. J., in the New England Historical and Genealogical Register for January, 1873.

Noah Hobart, ye last husband of my Great Grand Mother, Priscilla Hobart, was a school teacher in Duxbury, Mass., having graduated at Harvard College in 1724, and become acquainted with Priscilla Thomas, a very interesting young girl, daughter of Caleb Thomas, a respectable citizen of that town. Their acquaintance ripened into an engagement, & mutual promise of marriage, whenever his circumstances w'd permit him to discharge ye debts he had contracted for his education.

While this understanding subsisted between them, & they were enjoying ye happy relation of affianced lovers, & calmly waiting for such improvement in their affairs as w'd justify their marriage, John Watson Esqr., of Plymouth, my Great Grand Father, being a Widower having seen Priscilla, was much pleas'd with her, although ye serious difference of nearly thirty years existed in their ages, he being about 50, & she 22 years old.

Being, however, thus charm'd with Priscilla, he proceeded to Duxbury & call'd on her parents, & made known to them his views & wishes in relation to Priscilla, & requested their consent to visit their daughter, with ye object of offering himself to her in marriage. They inform'd M'r Watson that Priscilla was engaged to Mr. Hobart, but they w'd call her & let her speak for herself, they seeming pleas'd with ye offer, as M'r Watson's circumstances were known to be very eligible.

Priscilla was call'd, & appear'd gratified with an offer from so rich a suitor, & observed that she w'd see Noah, & talk with him about it. She convers'd with Noah, and he thought that, upon ye whole, it was not advisable for her to lose so good an opportunity; & as he was still so much in debt for his education, that it was quite uncertain when he w'd be able to relieve himself from his embarrassments, & be in a condition to marry her.

She then concluded to accept M'r Watson's offer; and in a few weeks he married her, & carried her to his home in Plymouth. In due time she bore him two sons, ye eldest, my great uncle William Watson; & ye youngest my grandfather Elkanah Watson; & soon after, in Sept. 1731, her husband died of a fever, and left his wife a handsome young widow, of about 25 years of age.

About ye same time that M'r Watson's death occurr'd, the wife of Thomas Lothrop Esqr., one of their neighbours, died, leaving a young infant, w'h was frequently sent to Mr's Watson to be nursed, she having also a nursing infant. In ye meantime, Noah Hobart, probably not having yet paid his college debts, did not now manifest any particular sentiments, or intentions in relation to her,

43

perhaps also being influenced by ye contrast in their condition, she being left a rich widow.

The intercourse created between M'r Lothrop (*) & Mr's Watson by their mutual interest in his nursing infant, brought about a reciprocal interest in each other, & in due time he offer'd, & was accepted by her as her second husband. She lived with him happily for some years, & bore him three children, (*) two sons & a daughter; viz. D'r Nathaniel Lothrop & Isaac Lothrop Esqr, of Plymouth, and Priscilla, married to Gershom Burr Esqr, of Connecticut; when M'r Lothrop died, & Priscilla became a widow for ye second time.

Noah Hobart, while ye incidents related in ye former chapter were occurring to Priscilla, having been settled in ye (Congregational) ministry at Fairfield, Connecticut, had married & his wife had died previously to the death of Mr. Lothrop. At a suitable interval, subsequent to these events, he concluded to make a visit to his first sweetheart, & went to Plymouth, & again proposed himself for her husband. She was very glad to see him & receiv'd him very graciously; and much regretted that she could not accept his proposals, without breaking a promise that she had made to M'r Lothrop on his deathbed, not to marry while his mother lived.

Noah, disappointed, set out for home with a heavy heart, & having reach'd Hingham, call'd on ye Revd M'r Shute, who invited him to stop & preach ye Thursday lecture for him; to w'h he assented. After ye lecture was over, as they were going home, they met a traveller on horseback, of whom M'r Shute enquired "where he was from?" He answered "from Plymouth;" when they further enquired "if there was any news?" He answered, "nothing particular, except that old Madam Lothrop died last night." Noah's face brightened up on this announcement, & he turned his face again towards Plymouth; and without being able to state any intervening particulars, we know that in three weeks "on that time, Priscilla married her third husband in ye person of her first lover, & was settled at Fairfield "ye minister's help-meet," & ye wife of ye Revd Noah Hobart

The life of Priscilla at Fairfield was tranquil and happy; & it is said that she sometimes confess'd to her children, in her old age, they

being also ye children of her other husbands, that ye period she lived with Noah was ye happiest portion of her life. She had no children by M'r Hobart. Her oldest son by M'r Lothrop, D'r Nathaniel Lothrop, married Ellen Hobart, ye daughter of Noah, and thus contributed further to cement this happy & long-deferr'd union. Priscilla, however, was destined to be a widow for ye third time, as ye Revd Noah Hobart died at Fairfield in ye year 1773, & left her in possession of his homestead there.

After ye death of M'r Hobart, Priscilla remained at Fairfield, occupying his house & receiving ye manifestations of ye affection and respect of his late Parish for a period of six years, until July, 1779, when ye whole village of Fairfield was burn'd by ye English troops under ye command of Govr Tryon.

Being now houseless she returned to Plymouth, & occupied ye house in w'h she had lived with her second husband, M'r Lothrop. She lived until 1796, nearly 10 years after this interview, & died in June of that year, aged 90 years.

Only four of the married women,
Elizabeth Hopkins, Eleanor Billington,
Susanna White Winslow, and Mary Brewster,
survived the first winter

James Kendall

Pastor For Sixty years

Rev. James Kendall, D.D.
Ordained 1 Jan. 1800.
Died 17 March 1859. Aged
89 years.
For sixty years Minister of
the First Parish in this
town.

My Peace I Give Unto You

"The Gift of God is Eternal Life"

James Kendall III graduated Harvard College 1796, ordained January 1, 1800, and for sixty years was minister of the First Parish Church, Plymouth. The Rev. Kendall was known as a "liberal preacher" whose theology tended toward what was to become known as "Unitarianism."

On Thanksgiving day November, 1799, at a meeting held for the election of a new pastor, twenty-three members of the church were in favor of Reverend James Kendal, the only candidate, while fifteen were in opposition. When the entire parish voted, two hundred and fifty-three favored Mr. Kendall, and fifteen were opposed. The schism was the first to occur over doctrinal matters in New England. In September, 1800, the conservative minority withdrew; and two years later they organized the society now known as the Church of the Pilgrimage.

He preached his last sermon on Thanksgiving-Day, November, 1857. Many contemporaries of Kendall agreed that he was called into the work of the ministry at a period when . . . "vice and infidelity abound, a time when the enemies of God are numerous, artful, and busy in their endeavors to overturn Christianity, and spread deism and atheism over the world".

First Parish Church in Plymouth is the oldest continuous church in New England.

This church has a long history of religious freedom and faith that dates back to the pilgrim landing and beyond.

They state:

"We trace our origin back to the year 1606 when a group of dissenters from the Church of England banded together in Scrooby. In 1620 part of the Leyden congregation set sail aboard the Mayflower, seeking the freedom to worship according to the dictates of their own conscience in the New World."

Massasoit in the Wampanoag language means "Great Leader." His real name was Ousamequin or "Yellow Feather"

Major William Bradford

Puritan Swamp Fighter

Major William Bradford was the son of William Bradford the second governor of Plymouth Colony who was elected to fill the vacancy caused by the death of John Carver, the first governor of the colony.

Major William Bradford commanded the Plymouth forces in the fight against the Narragansett Indians in the King Philip War. It was at the Great Swamp Fight where he was wounded by a musket ball which he carried the rest of his life.

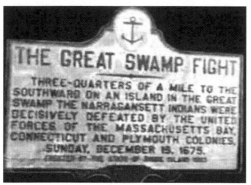

He married 3 times and had fifteen children.

He served as Deputy Governor of Plymouth in 1682-1686 and again in 1689-1692. During these terms from 1680 he also served as Treasurer. He was the Councillor of State to Gov. Sir Edmund Andros during the interim, 1687-1689.

A Disastrous Wreck

Brigantine General Arnold

Some monuments are quite specific as to the event that occurred but often only peak ones curiosity as to the actual happenings.
Such a monument can be found on the extreme southwesterly edge of Old Burial Hill near the Russell Street parking lot and Old Powder House.

The inscriptions reads:

In memory of Seventy two Seamen who perished
in Plymouth harbour on the 26, and 27,
days of December 1778, on board the private armed Brig, Gen. Arnold,
of twenty guns, James Magee of Boston, Commander,
sixty of whom were buried on this spot.

On the northwesterly side: –
Capt. James Magee died in Roxbury,
February 4, 1801; aged 51 years.

On the southwesterly side: –
Oh! falsely flattering were yon billows smooth
When forth, elated, sailed in evil hour,
That vessel whose disastrous fate, when told,
Fill'd every breast with sorrow and each eye
With piteous tears.

On the southeasterly side: –
This monument marks the resting place of
sixty of the seventy two mariners, "who perished
in their strife with the storm," and is erected by Stephen Gale of Portland,
Maine, a stranger to them, as a just memorial
of their sufferings and death.

49

The Story Behind the Monument

It was Christmas 1778, and snow was falling upon Boston Harbor. The brigantine General Arnold, named for the gallant hero of Quebec, was at anchor off Nantasket Road. In the early dawn, she set sail for the Carolinas, alongside the privateer Revenge.

The Arnold carried 21 guns, a detachment of Marines, and a cargo of military supplies for the American troops who were attempting to stop the British from cutting off the South from the Northern colonies. Her commander was Captain James Magee, an Irish born American patriot, who was looking forward to meeting up with the British, his lieflong enemy. Before the day was over, however, he would lose his ship to a greater enemy, the enraged sea.

Of the 105 men and boys who sailed with him, 81 would die a horrible death, and the others, all but himself, would be crippled for life. Under full sail, the privateers headed across Massachusetts Bay toward the open sea. The wind picked up, the snow fell harder, and soon they were in the midst of a Nor'East blizzard. Captain Barrows of the Revenge decided to ride out the storm off Cape Cod. Magee felt that his ship could weather the storm better in Plymouth Harbor behind Gurnet Point. But, the Arnold's anchor wouldn't hold, and she began to drift into the long harbor.

Magee had his men dismount 16 of the deck cannons and store them below to add weight to the hull and give the vessel stability. Her sails were furled and to the topmost struck, but nothing seemed to stop The Arnold's dragging anchor. Huge waves broke over the bow and quickly turned to ice.

The anchor cable broke and the Arnold sailed backwards into the harbor, bumped over a sand bar, and scraped to a sudden stop on top of a shallow water sand flat, only a mile from shore.

At first, Magee and his men thought they could lighten the vessel and slide her over the flat to shore. With axes,

50

they cut down her masts, but the heavy hull was already sinking into the sand, cracking her boards and leaking salt water into her hold. Icy waves washed over her main deck and the captain later reported "The quarter deck was the only place that could afford the most distant prospect of safety." Magee went on to say "Within a few hours, presented a scene that would shock the least delicate humanity. Some of my people were stifled to death with the snow, others perished with the extremity of the cold, and a few were washed off the deck and drowned."

There were a few bottles and casks of wine and brandy in the cargo. Some of the crew members ventured below into the half flooded hold to drown themselves in liquid warmth. Some were drunk before Captain Magee realized they had broken into the stores. He pleaded with them to pour the brandy into their shoes to prevent frostbite, instead of drinking it. Some obeyed, but those who did not were dead by the next morning. Those huddled together on the quarterdeck, their clothes first drenched then frozen to their bodies, covered themselves with the sails for protection from the salt spray and the snow. By the morning of the 26th, thirty of them were frozen to death. The blizzard continued. Magee could see but a shadow of land through the falling snow, so he fired his signal gun in hopes of getting the attention of the people of the town. Three crewmen managed to launch the privateers long boat into the wild sea, then started rowing to shore, but they were lost sight of and never heard from again.

Late in the afternoon when there was a short break in the storm, the people of Plymouth sent dories out from shore, however, none of them could make it to the stranded vessel. They decided that the only way to the Arnold was to build a causeway of ice and snow one mile long out to the sand flat. Working throughout the night, through the next day and night, the people of Plymouth accomplished what seemed impossible - they built a road out to the distressed privatee.

Meanwhile the shipwreck victims spent a second and third night on the quarter-deck in sub-freezing temperatures. The living feared going to sleep, knowing that if they did, they probably would not wake up again. In an attempt to block out wind and waves, they piled the dead bodies of their comrades around them. The Arnold sank deeper into the sand, knee deep water now covering the main deck. In an effort to keep his remaining crewmen and Marines alive, Captain Magee requested, then demanded, that the men keep walking around and exercising on the little deck in order to maintain their circulation.

He was especially anxious about two boys aboard: Connie Marchang, age 10 and Barney Downs, age 15. Magee prodded them to walk in place even though they were both so exhausted and frozen they could hardly stand. He urged them over and over agin not to give up. Marchant later said, "I ascribe my preservation mainly to the reiterated efforts of Captain Magee." On Monday morning, December 28th when the causeway was completed, the people of Plymouth passed over the ice to the wreck. "It was a scene unutterably awful and distressing, writes Plymouth's Doctor Thatcher. "The ship was sunk ten feet in the sand; the waves had been for about thirty six hours sweeping the main deck, and even here they were obliged to pile together dead bodies to make room for the living. Seventy dead bodies, frozen in to all imaginable postures, were strewn over the deck, or attached to shrouds and spars; about thirty exhibited signs of life, but were unconscious whether in life or death. The bodies remained in the posture in which they died, the features dreadfully distorted. Some were erect, some bending forward, some sitting with the head resting on the knees, and some with both arms extended, clinging to spars or some part of the vessel."
Sleds and slabs of wood were used to carry the survivors and the stiffened corpses over the ice road to shore. The dead were piled in the Plymouth Courthouse, the living brought to local homes to spend agonizing hours thawing out.

Magee skippered merchant ships out of Salem for the remainder of his life, including the famous Astrea that opened American trade with China. Whenver in home port at Christmas, Magee called for a reunion of the 24 Arnold survivors, assisting any who were destitute with a gift from his own wages. At his request, when he died, he was buried with the Arnold crew at Burial Hill, Plymouth, MA..

Author unknown

Civil War Brother Casualties

George Wadsworth of Co. E. 29th Mass. Reg,. died at Crab Orchard, KY Aug. 31 1863 aged 35 years & 8 months

Charles Wadsworth of Co. E 39h Mass Reg. who died as a prisoner of war at Salisbury, NC Nov. 10, 1864 aged 31 years and 4 months

Capt. Joseph W. Collingwood, Co. H. 18th Reg. Mass. Vols. Wounded at the battle of Fredericksburg, VA Dec 13, 1862; died Dec. 24th 1862 aged 41 years

Corp. Thomas Collingwood, Co. E 29th Mass. died at Crab Orchard, KY Aug. 31, 1863, aged 32 years, 9 months and 21 days

Nathaniel Morton

Keeper of the Records - Plymouth Colony's first published historian

Nathaniel Morton, b 1613 in Lyden Holland d June 29, 1685. He came to Plymouth with his father in 1623 on the ship *Ann.* In 1645 he was elected clerk of the Colony court, and remained in office until his death. He was nephew of Governor Bradford and as such was uniquely qualified to chronicle colonial life as he had access to his uncle's papers, as well as to the archives of the colony. In 1669 he published *New England's Memorial,* a book frequently referred to as 'the cornerstone' of New England history.

He also wrote the *First Beginnings and After Progress of the Church of Christ at Plymouth, in New England,* which preserved the early history of the first church established in New England.

"Mr Nathaniel Morton Secretary of Plymouth Colony and a pilar in the Church here deceased June 29 1685 Being Entred in o the Seventy third yeare of his age".

Forefathers Monument
Prototype for the Statue of Liberty

The cornerstone was laid in 1858 and the statue completed in 1889. The monument stands 81 feet high and is the largest solid granite statue in America.

It cost $150,000 with funds from the Federal Government, the Commonwealth of Massachusetts, the State of Connecticut and 11,000 individuals including a $10 donated by then president Abraham Lincoln.

The illustrator of "Uncle Tom's Cabin," world famous Boston artist Hammatt Billings, also designed Forefathers Monument.

The massive figure of Faith with her foot upon Plymouth Rock towers above the four seated figures below: Liberty, Law, Education and Morality. Beneith the seated figures are four marble alto-reliefs representing significant events in Pilgrim History: the Departure from Holland, the Signing of the Compact, the Landing at Plymouth and the Treaty with Massasoit.

By LANE LAMBERT
The Patriot Ledger

In the spring of 1861, there was little on President Abraham Lincoln's mind besides the Civil War.

Fort Sumter had been attacked. As the first Union volunteers gathered in and around Washington, Confederate forces formed in nearby Virginia, and the border states of Maryland and Kentucky threatened to join the secession.

Bridgewater State College history professor and Lincoln scholar Thomas Turner unearthed this obscure episode in Lincoln's life as he researched online records of the Library of Congress.

Two panels are dedicated to those who arrived in 1620 and 1621 and a third contains this quotation:

"As one small candle may light a thousand, so the light here kindled hath shown unto many, yea, in some sort to our whole nation, let the glorious name of Jehovah have all the praise."

--Gov. William Bradford

Holocaust in Ireland

640 United Irishmen Slain

Picture courtesy of rootsweb.com

CROPPIES GRAVES GRAIGUECULLEN, IRELAND

The Croppies Grave at 98 Street, Graiguecullen is the last resting place for the 640 United Irishmen who died in action in the early morning of 25th May 1798 in what is now called the Tullow Street Holocaust

The United Irishmen were betrayed by one of their own leaders, a James Keogh a/k/a "Yellow Jim", and fell into a well planned ambush. They were mowed down by shot and shell or smoked out of their places of refuge and butchered like hunted animals.

The memory of the United Irishmen is honored by the '98 Street Monument. The wall and railings of the grave were paid for with funds raised by the GAA. The memorial slab is the gift of an Orangeman, Rowan McCoombe. The inscription on the slab reads:

"To the memory of the 640 United Irishmen who fell in Tullow Street, 25 May1798"

From 'Fiacc's Folk' Parish Magazine in the 1997/98 edition

Irish Freedom Fighter and Holocaust Survivor in Exile?

Shipwreck of the Hibernia

ANDREW FARRELL,
of respectable connexions
In IRELAND Aged 38 years,
Owner & Commander of the
Ship Hibernia, Sailed from
Boston Jany 26, And was
wrecked on Plymouth Beach
Jany 29 1805. His remains
With five of seven seaman
Who perished with him are
here interred.O piteous lot of
man's uncertain state! What
woes on life's eventful
journey wait--By sea what
treacherous calms; what
sudden storms; And death
attendant in a thousand
forms.

Was our Andrew Farrell the same Andrew Farrell who, seven years earlier, was called Captain by the rebels during Tullow Street Holocaust of 1798?

Writings in 1801 state that. . . "Andrew Farrell had a sword in his hand and was called Captain by the rebels. He desired the loyalists to fall on their knees and prepare for death as they should be killed directly ..."

Is his connection with the Irish freedom fighters what is meant by respectable connexions in Ireland?

From County Carlow Genealogy 2004

Early Grave Stone Carvers

Nehemiah Burbank

Nehemiah and his older brother Samuel were both among the earliest stone cutters in the Plymouth area. They are credited with sixty eight gravestones. Two are in Plymouth and only one is on Old Burial Hill. That stone is in memory of their grandfather, Timothy Burbank, who was a tailor in Plymouth and lived to be ninety years of age.

Timothy Burbank

The brothers were apprentices of Plymouth's Master Carver Lemuel Savery. Their grandfather Timothy's stone is reported to be one of the brothers earliest works

---

Lobsters, clams, and mussels were considered "hard rations" when the food supply was low. Many Pilgrims thought that lobsters were fit only for pigs!

Revd. Chandler Robbins D D

There were NO PILGRIMS at the first Thanksgiving!

This Stone Consecrated to the
memory
Of the Revd Chandler Robbins D D
was erected By the inhabitants of
the first Religious Society in Plymouth
As their last grateful tribute of
respect For his eminent labors In the
ministry of JESUS CHRIST
Which commenced January 30th 1760
And continued till his death June
30th 1799 Ætatis 61 When he
entered into the everlasting rest
Prepared for the faithful
ambassadors Of the most high God.

*Ah come heaven's radiant Offspring
hither throngBehold your prophet
your Elijah tied
Let sacred symphony attune each
tongueTo chant hosannahs with the
virtuous dead.*

It was not until 1793, 175 years after the Colonists landed, that the name "Pilgrims" was applied to the colonists. In that year, on the celebration of "Forefathers Day" at Plymouth, the Reverend Chandler Robbins, who preached the sermon, used the term. In the sermon, Robbins read a letter written by William Bradford. Bradford's letter described how 101 passengers mustered up the courage to board the Mayflower and begin a treacherous three month voyage to a virtually unknown land. Bradford commented, "They knew they were pilgrims and looked not much on those things, but lifted up their eyes to the heavens, their dearest country, and quieted their spirits." Based on this, Pr. Robbins started calling this band of pioneers, Pilgrims. The name stuck.

America's First Naval War
Fought Without a Navy

Plymouth Sea Captains to the Rescue

The Continental Navy had been disbanded in 1785. In 1790 the first US Congress establish - ed the "Cutters" primarily to enforce tariffs and in 1798 congress established the US Navy.

Therefore between 1785 and 1798 America did not have a navy.

Quasi-War with France (1797-1801)
By June of 1797 the French had captured 316 American ships and their cargo. The value of the cargo was estimated to be worth 15 million dollars.

In response, the U.S. government authorized 365 privateers to war against French ships in the Americas. About 120 of the privateers were from New England and it would follow that scores of the captains hailed from Plymouth as Plymouth was a major maritime center at the time.

As you walks through Plymouth's Old Burial Hill Cemetery, you have to be impressed by the large number of sea captains buried there and, as you pass their numerous gravestones, wonder just how many of them participated in America's first naval war fought without a navy.

Thomas W HAYDEN

Hewas the third member of Co. E 29th Mass. from Plymouth to be killed at Crab Orchard, Kentucky. He died on September 1, 1863. Both Corporal Thomas Collingwood and George Wadsworth perished a day earlier.

Thomas W HAYDEN

Co. E29 Mass Vol
Died
Sept. 1, 1863
At Crab Orchard, Kentucky
Aged 33 years
& 2 months

A letter from the Front

Below is a letter written a few days earlier describing the conditions in the area.

Camp Near Crab Orchard Ky
Aug 20th
Dear Father"We have started on our great march over the mountains and have marched 2 days since one day was the hardest day I ever marched it was so intinely it was almost suffacating there was several men droped down in the road just as though they were dead and layed so for hours Harvy was almost as bad off as any of them Metts & I came very near being we fell out and it was the first time I ever fell but I had to cave we layed side of the road untill it got cooler then we started on it was all foolishness We are all well now and do not feel any thing of it the sweat run off from me in streams almost it is very warm here more so then it is up in O I tell you what it is it is hard to see men drop down in the road from heat but they fell thick around me."
Excerpts from a letter H. E. Randall dated August 20, 1863 to his father.

Lieut. Frederick Holmes

Frederick Holmes, Lieut.
38 Mass. Vol Infantry, aged 28 years, Killed June 14th 1863 while leading his men to the assault on the enemy's works at Fort Hudson, LA
In cooperation with Maj. Gen. Ulysses S. Grant's offensive against Vicksburg, Union Maj. Gen. Nathaniel P. Banks' army moved against the Confederate stronghold at Port Hudson on the Mississippi River.

On May 27, after their frontal assaults were repulsed, the Federals settled into a siege which lasted for 48 days. Banks renewed his assaults on June 14 but the defenders successfully repelled them. On July 9, 1863, after hearing of the fall of Vicksburg, the Confederate garrison of Port Hudson surrendered, opening the Mississippi River to Union navigation from its source to New Orleans.

General McClellan's slow movements, combined with General Lee's escape, and continued raiding by Confederate cavalry, dismayed many in the North. On November 7, Lincoln replaced McClellan with Major-General Ambrose E. Burnside. Burnside's forces were defeated in a series of attacks against entrenched Confederate forces at Fredericksburg, Virginia, and Burnside was replaced with General Joseph Hooker.

On November 14, Burnside, now in command of the Army of the Potomac, sent a corps to occupy the vicinity of Falmouth near Fredericksburg. The rest of the army soon followed. Lee reacted by entrenching his army on the heights behind the town.

On December 11, Union engineers laid five pontoon bridges across the Rappahannock under fire. On the 12th, the Federal army crossed over, and on December 13, Burnside mounted a series of futile frontal assaults on Prospect Hill and Marye's Heights that resulted in staggering casualties. Meade's division, on the Union left flank, briefly penetrated Jackson's line but was driven back by a counterattack.

Union generals C. Feger Jackson and George Bayard, and Confederate generals Thomas R.R. Cobb and Maxey Gregg were killed. On December 15, Burnside called off the offensive and recrossed the river, ending the campaign. Burnside initiated a new offensive in January 1863, which quickly bogged down in the winter mud. The abortive "Mud March" and other failures led to Burnside's replacement by Maj. Gen. Joseph Hooker in January 1863.

Number of Veterans buried on Old Burial Hill

Revolutionary War	79
War of 1812	12
Civil War	48
Total	139

US Presidents with Mayflower Heritage

John Adams — *John Alden & William Mullins*
The first Vice President became the second President of the United States. His opponent in the election, Thomas Jefferson, had won the second greatest number of electoral votes and therefore had been elected Vice President by the Electoral College. Chief Justice Oliver Ellsworth administered the oath of office in the Hall of the House of Representatives in Federal Hall before a joint session of Congress.

John Quincy Adams — *John Alden & William Mullins*
He was the 6th president of the United States and was the son of John Adams, 2d president. *Independence* and *Union* were the watchwords of his career; a "Union of the United States of North America" to grow by the destiny of Providence and nature to become a continental republic of free citizens stretching from ocean to ocean and from Gulf to Arctic."

James A. Garfield — *John Billington*
As the last of the log cabin Presidents, James A. Garfield attacked political corruption and won back for the Presi-dency a measure of prestige it had lost during the Reconstruction period.
He was born in Cuyahoga County, Ohio, in 1831. Fatherless at two, he later drove canal boat teams, somehow earning enough money for an education. He was graduated from Williams College in Massachusetts in 1856.

Zachary Taylor — *William Brewster & Isaac Allerton*
He was the 12th president of the United States.
In 1849 Taylor reluctantly agreed to efforts to admit California to the Union as a free state.

Mortified by scandals involving trusted cabinet members, he was determined to reorganize the cabinet. Unfortunately, while attending the opening ceremony for the construction of the Washington Monument on the forth of July 1850, he consumed food spoiled by the noonday heat. He suffered acute gastroenteritis and died five days later.

Ulysses Grant — *Richard Warren*
Ulysses S. Grant was 18th president of the United States and the general-in-chief of the Union (Northern) forces in the U.S. Civil War, and was a hero in the North for his victories in key battles during the war.

Franklin Delano Roosevelt — *Isaac Allerton, Francis Cooke*
Franklin D. Roosevelt served longer in office than any other president. He broke the tradition that limited presidents to two terms and was elected to four consecutive terms.

George Herbert Walker Bush — John Howland, Francis Cooke and John Tilley

He was elected the 41st president of the United States on Nov. 8, 1988, and inaugurated on Jan. 20, 1989. He had held an array of senior public positions and served (1981–89) as Ronald Reagan's vice- president, becoming the first sitting vice-president to be elected in his own right since Martin Van Buren in 1836.

George W. Bush — *John Howland, Francis Cooke, Henry Samson, and John Tilley*
He is the 43rd President of the United States. He was elected to serve two terms, 2001 -2008. Prior to his Presidency, President Bush served for 6 years as the 46th Governor of the State of Texas.

First Ladies and a Vice President with Mayflower connections

Barbara Bush — *John Howland & Henry Samson*
Barbara Pierce met her future husband, George Bush, when she was 16. She left Smith College after two years to marry him in 1945. They moved to Texas, where the Bushes raised four sons and a daughter; another daughter died of leukemia at age three.

Dan Quayle — *Myles Standish, John Alden & William Mullins*
Representative and a Senator from Indiana and a Vice President of the United States; born in Indianapolis, Marion County, Ind., February 4, 1947; attended the public schools of Phoenix, Ariz., and Huntington, Ind.; graduated, DePauw University, Greencastle, Ind., 1969; graduated, Indiana University, Indianapolis 1974; admitted to the Indiana bar in 1974; served in the Indiana National Guard 1969-1975.

Lucretia (Rudolph) Garfield -- *Mary Chilton, James Chilton*
Lucretia Rudolph and James Garfield married on Nov. 11, 1858. They had seven children. Her husband was inaugurated in March 1881. President Garfield was shot by an assassin. He died in September.

Edith Roosevelt -- Mrs. Theodore Roosevelt -- *Desire Howland, JOHN Howland*
She was born at Norwich, CT in 1861 and married Theodore Roosevelt in 1886 following the death of his first wife in 1884. The assassination of William McKinley in 1901 brought the Roosevelts to the White House where they remained until 1909.

67

Mayflower Royalty and Pilgrim Bigamist

Richard More. . . The bigamist royal pilgrim

HERE
LYETH BURIED
Ye BODY OF
CAPT. RICHARD MORE
AGED 84 YEARS
DIED 1692
A MAYFLOWER
PILGRIM

Mayflower Pilgrim Buried in Salem

Richard More's gravestone still survives, and is the only known original gravestone still in existence which was erected at the time of burial. It was vandalized around 1919 when someone carved the incorrect "died 1692" onto it and later added "Mayflower Pilgrim."

His stone is in Burial Point (the old Charter Street Cemetery), located between Charter and Darby Streets in Salem, Massachusetts. The original marker, triangular at the top, is now strengthened by an encasement of slate. Buried on either side of him are his first and second wives

Richard More and his three siblings were abandoned by their mother and cast out of England by their "father," Commander Samuel More. Three of the four children perished upon reaching the New World. On December 6, 1620, Richard's brother Jasper More died on board the *Mayflower* while still in Provincetown Harbor. He was the first to die in the new world. Shortly thereafter, his sisters Ellen and Mary died. Our subject, Richard More, now found himself alone in the New World, without parents or siblings.

Why would parents cast their young children away?

Commander Samuel More, the children's', father was married at the tender age of 16 to his third cousin Katherine More, the heiress of Larden, then 23, presumably in order to keep the estate in the family. Four children were born and baptized as Samuel's before he became aware of "the common fame of the adulterous life of said Katherine More with one Jacob Blakeway."

Subsequent to divorce proceeding by Katherine and her rejection of the children, Samuel ultimately arranged with *"honest and religious people"* (Carver, Winslow and Brewster of the Mayflower) to: *"Transport them into the new world; to see that they were properly lodged, maintained fed and clothed; that at the end of seven years they should have 50 acres apiece."* It was his desire to remove them from *"these partes,"* where *"great blotts and blemishes may fall upon them."* Sadly only Richard survived the treacherous journey.

Descended from Kings

With a marred paternal heritage and a mother who callously abandoned him, Richard nevertheless arrived in the New World with a heritage that traced to royalty. The More were direct descendants of King Malcolm III of Scotland, King Edward I of England, and King Henry II of England, Alfred the Great and Charlemagne.

He therefore, is the only Mayflower pilgrim of royal blood to marry and have a family in the new world. Richard and his first wife Christian had seven children.

Bigamy in Puritan New England?

Around 1627 Richard More, a boy of about thirteen years of age, left the Rev. Brewster's family and returned to England. He returned in 1635 with the woman who would soon become his first wife, Christian Hunter. The couple moved to Salem where Richard became a sea captain. Recent discoveries by Robert M. Sherman, FASG indicate that on 23 October 1645, Richard More, while still married to Christian, married

70

Elizabeth Woolno at St. Duncan's, Stepney, Middlesex, England, effectively having two wives, one on each side of the ocean.

Richard joined the First Church of Salem and became a freeman in 1643 and records there give a glimpse into Richard's character and habits. Salem Church Records do record:

"Old Captain More having been for many years under suspicion and common fame of lasciviousness, and some degree at least of incontency . . . but for want of proof we could go no further. He was at last left to himself so farr as that he was convicted before justices of peace by three witnesses of gross unchastity with another mans wife and was censured by them."

The Old Captain repented of this in 1691, and the Church officially forgave him. Richard More died in Salem sometime between 1693 and 1696. Therefore Richard More would have witnessed the 1692 Salem witchcraft hysteria.

Richard More facts:
One of two male children on the *Mayflower* who started family lines in America and yet were too young to sign the *Mayflower Compact*.

1. Only Mayflower passenger whose place of burial is marked by a gravestone laid at the exact time of burial.
2. Only surviving Mayflower passenger with royal heritage
3. Only Puritan known to be a bigamist

Longest surviving male of the original *Mayflower* company, only Mary (Allerton) Cushman lived longer, dying in December of 1699

Governor William Bradford

Born in Austerfield, Yorkshire, England, in March, 1588; died May 9, 1657.

He was elected governor in 1621 upon the death of John Carver. He was reelected governor 30 times and was governor for most of his life, except for the five years he chose not to serve. Even then he was elected assistant governor.

Bradford chronicles of Pilgrim life and commerce provide us a unique insight and history of the Plymouth Colony. Perhaps the most valuable of Bradford's writings was his 270 page "History of the Plymouth Plantation." It also included the history of the society from its inception in 1602 till the time when it departed for America in 1620, and its history in Plymouth down to 1647.

Dorothy Bradford, age 20, fell off the *Mayflower* anchored in Provincetown Harbor and drowned while her husband William was away exploring in the shallop. She never saw Plymouth.

Early Pastors and Elders of the first church of Plymouth

Pastors

Name	Time Period
Ralph Smith,	*1629–1635*
John Reyner,	*1636–1654*
John Cotton,	*1669–1697*
Ephraim Little,	*1699–1723*
Nathaniel Leonard,	*1724–1760*
Chandler Robbins	*1760–1799*
James Kendall,	*1800–1859*
Edward Henry Hall,	*1859–1867*

Associate Pastors

George Ware Briggs,	*1838–1852*
Henry Lewis Myrick,	*1853–1854*
George S. Ball,	*1855–1857*
Edward Henry Hall,	*1859–1859*

Elders

William Brewster,	*1620–1644*
Thomas Cushman,	*1649–1691*
Thomas Faunce,	*1699–1746*

The *Fortune* 1621

The ship Fortune arrived at Plymouth on November 9, 1621, just a few weeks after the First Thanksgiving. This passenger list is based on the 1623 Division of Land, the passenger list compiled by Charles Edward Banks in Planters of the Commonwealth, and by the information found in Eugene Aubrey Stratton's Plymouth Colony: Its History and its People, 1620-1691.

Fortune Passenger List

John Adams	Martha Ford (daughter)
William Basset	John Ford (son)
Elizabeth Basset (Wife)	Robert Hickes
William Beale	William Hilton
Jonathan Brewster	Bennet Morgan
Elizabeth Basset (Wife)	Thomas Morton
Clement Briggs	Austen Nicolas
Edward Bumpas	William Palmer
John Cannon	William Palmer (son)
William Conner	William Pitt
Robert Cushman	Thomas Prence
Thomas Cushman (Son)	Moses Simonson
Philipe de la Noye	Hugh Statie
Steven Deane	James Steward
Thomas Flavell & Son	William Tench
_____ Ford	John Winslow
Martha Ford (Wife)	William Wright
Thomas Flavell & Son	

Brradford transcribed his memory of the first Colony in his book titled "Of Plimoth Plantation." The original manuscript is held in the Massachusetts State archives

The Ships *Anne* and *Little James 1623*

The Anne arrived in Plymouth in July, 1623 accompanied by the *Little James,* bringing new settlers along with many of the wives and children that had been left behind in Leyden when the *Mayflower* departed in 1620. This ship passenger list is reconstructed from the 1623 Division of Lands, the passenger list compiled by Charles Banks in *Planters of the Commonwealth*, and the research found in Eugene Aubrey Stratton's *Plymouth Colony: Its History and Its People, 1620-1691.*

- Annable, Anthony
  - Jane (Momford) Annable, wife
  - Sarah Annable, daughter
  - Hannah Annable, daughter
- Bangs, Edward
- Bartlett, Robert
- Buckett, Mary
- Brewster, Patience
  - Fear Brewster, sister
- Clarke, Thomas
- Conant, Christopher
- Cooke, Mrs. Hester (Mahieu)
  - Jane Cooke, daughter
  - Jacob Cooke, son
  - Hester Cooke, daughter
- Dix, Anthony
- Faunce, John
- Flavel, Mrs. Elizabeth
- Flood, Edmond
- Fuller, Mrs. Bridget (Lee)
- Godbertson, Godbert
  - Sarah (Allerton)(Vincent)(Priest) Godbertson, wife
  - Samuel Godbertson, son
  - Sarah Priest, step-daughter
  - Mary Priest, step-daughter
- Hatherly, Timothy
- Heard, William

Hicks, Mrs. Margaret Samuel Hicks, son

Anne and *Little James 1623 Continued*

- o Lydia Hicks, daughter
- • Hilton, Mrs. William
- o William Hilton, son
- o Mary Hilton, daughter
- • Holman, Edward
- • Kempton, Manasseh
- • Long, Robert
- • Mitchell, Experience
- • Morton, George
- o Juliana Morton, wife
- o Nathanial Morton, son
- o John Morton, son
- o Ephraim Morton, son
- o Patience Morton, daughter
- o Sarah Morton, daughter
- • Morton, Thomas Jr.
- • Newton, Ellen
- • Oldham, John
- o Mrs. Oldham, wife
- o Lucretia Oldham, sister
- • Palmer, Mrs. Frances
- • Penn, Christian
- • Pierce, Abraham
- • Pratt, Joshua
- • Rand, James
- • Rattliff, Robert
- o Mrs. Rattliff, wife
- • Snow, Nicholas
- • Southworth, Alice (Carpenter)
- • Sprague, Francis
- o Anna Sprague, wife
- o Mercy Sprague, daughter
- • Standish, Mrs. Barbara
- • Tilden, Thomas
- o (?) Tilden, wife
- o child Tilden
- • Tracy, Stephen
- • Wallen, Ralph
- o Joyce Wallen, wife
- • Warren, Mrs. Elizabeth
- o Mary Warren, daughter
- o Elizabeth Warren, daughter
- o Anna Warren, daughter
- o Sarah Warren, daughter il Warren, daughter

76

Revolutionary War Veterans on Old Burial Hill   Denotes Casualty *

Name	Section
Seth Churchill	A
James Warren	A
Eleazer Holmes	A
Icabod Holmes Jr.	A
Richard Bagnell	A
Lemuel Simmons	A
Nathaniel Carver	A
Capt Thomas Doten	B
William Watson Jr	B
David Turner	B
Job Foster *	B
Capt. Richard Cooper	B
Nathaniel Bradford	B
Lemuel Bradford	B
Isaac Churchill	B
Nathaniel Morton	B
Josiah Cotton	B
Joseph Trask	B
Samuel Sherman	B
James Thacher MD	B
Thomas Morton	B
Lemuel Robbins	B
Seth Morton	B
Deacon Solomon Churchill	B
Thomas Bartlett	B
William Persons	B
John Bartlett	B
Samuel Churchill	B
Ezra Finney	B
Elijah Dunham	B
Seth Rider	B
Capt Rufus Robbins	B
Nathaniel Ripley	CW
Ebenezer N Bradford	CW
Samuel N Holmes	CW
Joseph Plaskett	CW
Barnabus Holmes	CW
Capt Simeon Sampson	CE
William Hueston	CE
General Nathaniel Goodwin	D
Capt Jacob Taylor	F
William Rider	F
Jacob Doten	F
Ebenezer Robins *	F
John Churchill	F
Peter Holmes	F

77

War of 1812 Veterans on Old Burial Hill

Benjamin Bagnell	A
Atwood Drew	B
Rufus Robins	B
James Howard	B
John H Clark	CE
Nathaniel Hueston	CE
Nathaniel Bradford	CW
Finney Leach	F
David Bradford	F
Isaac LeBarron	M
James Kendall	?
Sylvanus Rogers	N

Revolutionary War Veterans on Old Burial Hill

Denotes Casualty *

Name	Section
Samuel Robbins	G
William Doten	G
Thomas S Howland *	G
Nathaniel Holmes	H F
Abraham Hammatt	
Timothy Goodwin	J
William Weston	K
Benjamin Rider	K
Thomas Jackson	K
Samuel Bartlett	K
William Bradford	K
William Keen	K
Lewis Weston	K
Theophilus Cotton	K
Charles Dyer	K
James E Stillman	K
Capt Jesse Harlow	L
Ammaziah Harlow	L
Jesse Harlow	L
Capt James Collins	L
Capt Magee	L
William Thomas, MD	L
Nathaniel Thomas	L
Joseph Bramhall	L
Capt Joseph Thomas	L
Capt William Bartlett	L
Stephen Paine	M
Ichabod Rogers	N
Capt James Doten	N
Capt Nathaniel Ellis	N
Capt John Paty	N

Mayflower Compact 1620

Agreement Between the Settlers at New Plymouth : 1620

IN THE NAME OF GOD, AMEN. We, whose names are underwritten, the Loyal Subjects of our dread Sovereign Lord King James, by the Grace of God, of Great Britain, France, and Ireland, King, Defender of the Faith, &c. Having undertaken for the Glory of God, and Advancement of the Christian Faith, and the Honour of our King and Country, a Voyage to plant the first Colony in the northern Parts of Virginia; Do by these Presents, solemnly and mutually, in the Presence of God and one another, covenant and combine ourselves together into a civil Body Politick, for our better Ordering and Preservation, and Furtherance of the Ends aforesaid: And by Virtue hereof do enact, constitute, and frame, such just and equal Laws, Ordinances, Acts, Constitutions, and Officers, from time to time, as shall be thought most meet and convenient for the general Good of the Colony; unto which we promise all due Submission and Obedience. IN WITNESS whereof we have hereunto subscribed our names at Cape-Cod the eleventh of November, in the Reign of our Sovereign Lord King James, of England, France, and

Mr. John Carver,	Mr. William Mullins,	Thomas Rogers,
Mr. William Bradford,	Mr. William White,	Thomas Tinker,
Mr Edward Winslow,	Mr. Richard Warren,	John Ridgdale
Mr. William Brewster.	John Howland,	Edward Fuller,
Isaac Allerton,	Mr. Steven Hopkins,	Richard Clark,
Myles Standish,	Digery Priest,	Richard Gardiner,
John Alden,	Thomas Williams,	Mr. John Allerton,
John Turner,	Gilbert Winslow,	Thomas English,
Francis Eaton,	Edmund Margesson,	Edward Doten,
James Chilton,	Peter Brown,	Edward Liester
John Craxton,	Richard Britteridge	
John Billington,	George Soule,	
Joses Fletcher,	Edward Tilly,	
John Goodman,	John Tilly,	
Mr. Samuel Fuller,	Francis Cooke,	
Mr. Christopher Martin.		

Mayflower Passenger

List of Survivor, their occupation and age

Fifty of the one hundred and two persons aboard the Mayflower when they left for the New World died shortly after arriving in Plymouth in November 1620. Nearly half of the survivors were children.

Mayflower Passengers	Occupation,	Age

(**Bold** indicates those who died the first winter.)

Alden, John	Cooper,	21
Allerton, Isaac	Tailor, merchant,	34
Allerton, Mary		
Bartholomew Allerton	Child between 7/8 years	
Remember Allerton	Child between 5/6 years	
Mary Allerton	Child between 3/4 years	
Allerton, John		
Billington, John		38
Billington, Elinor		
John Billington	Child of 16 years	
Francis Billington	Child of 14 years	
Bradford, William	Cloth maker,	30
Bradford, Dorothy		
Brewster, William	Printer,	54
Brewster, Mary		
Love Brewster	Child of 13 years	
Wrestling Brewster	Child of 9 years	
Britteridge, Richard	The first to die in Plymouth	

Mayflower Passengers	Occupation,	Age
Brown, Peter		20
Butten, William ("youth")		Dies at sea
Carter, Robert		
Carver, John		
Carver, Katherine		
___, Dorothy Maidservant of John and Katherine Carver		
Chilton, James		
Chilton, Susanna		
Mary Chilton	Child aged 13	
Clarke, Richard		
Cooke, Francis	Wool comber,	37
John Cooke	Child aged 15	
Cooper, Humility	Child of 1 year	
Crackstone, John		
John Crackstone	Child of 18 years	
Doty, Edward	Servant to Stephen Hopkins,	21
Eaton, Francis	Carpenter,	25
Eaton, Sarah		
Samuel Eaton	Child of 1 year	
Ely, _____	(seaman, hired to stay a year)	
English, Thomas		
Fletcher, Moses		
Fuller, Edward		
Fuller, _____ (wife of Edward Fuller)		
Samuel Fuller	Child aged 12	
Fuller, Samuel	Surgeon	
Gardiner, Richard	Seaman,	38
Goodman, John		
Holbeck, William		
Hooke, John		
Hopkins, Stephen	Tanner,	38
Hopkins, Elizabeth		

Mayflower Passengers	Occupation, Age
Constance Hopkins	Child of 13 years
Giles Hopkins	Child of 11 years
Damaris Hopkins	Child of 2 years
Oceanus Hopkins &. Nov. 1620	born at sea between Sept
Howland, John	Servant to John Carver, 21
Langmore, John	
Latham, William	Child of 11 years
Lester, Edward Servant to Stephen Hopkins, 18 years	
Margesson, Edmund	
Martin, Christopher	
Martin, Marie	
Minter, Desire	Child of 15 years
More, Ellen	
More, Jasper Died while at anchor off Cape Cod	
More, Mary	
More, Richard	Child of 6 years
Mullins, William	
Mullins, Alice	
Joseph Mullins	
Priscilla Mullins	Aged 17 years
Priest, Degory	
Prower, Solomon	
Rigsdale, John	
Rigsdale, Alice	
Rogers, Thomas	
Joseph Rogers	Aged 17 years
Sampson, Henry	Aged 16 years
Soule, George	Servant to Edward Winslow

Mayflower Passengers	Occupation,	Age
Edward Winslow,		21
Standish, Myles	Military Captain,	27
Standish, Rose		
Story, Elias		
Thompson, Edward	Died while at anchor off Cape Cod	
Tilley, Edward		
Tilley, Agnes		
Tilley, John		
Tilley, Joan		
Elizabeth Tilley	Aged 15 years	
Tinker, Thomas		
Tinker ____ (wife of Thomas Tinker)		
____ Tinker (son)		
Trevor, William	Seaman, hired to stay a year	
Turner, John		
____ Turner (son, 5)		
____ Turner (son, 3)		
Warren, Richard	Merchant,	42
White, William		
White, Susanna		
Resolved White	Aged 5 years	
Peregrine White	Born while at anchor off Cape Cod	
Wilder, Roger		
Williams, Thomas		
Winslow, Edward	Printer,	25
Winslow, Elizabeth		
Winslow, Gilbert	Aged 20 years	

Familiar names
with Mayflower Roots

John Ellis "Jeb" Bush — *John Howland, Francis Cooke, John Tilley and Henry Samson*
Florida Governor
Henry Cabot Lodge, Jr. — *John Howland*
U.S. Senator from Massachusetts
Cokie Roberts — *Elder William Brewster*
Political Analyst for ABC and NPR
Bing Crosby — *William Brewster*
comedian, film star & singer
Ralph Waldo Emerson — *John Howland & John Tilley*
poet
Hugh Hefner — *William Bradford*
founder of Playboy Magazine
Henry Wadsworth Longfellow — *John Howland*
poet
Marilyn Monroe — *John Alden & William Mullins*
actress
Anna Mary Robertson "Grandma" Moses — *Francis Cooke*
20th century American primitive painter
Lillian Russell — *John Howland*
stage & film actress
Alan B. Shepard, Jr. — *Richard Warren*
first American in space and fifth man to walk on the moon
Joseph Smith — *John Howland*
founder, The Church of Jesus Christ of Latter-day Saints
Noah Webster — *William Bradford*
author of the first American dictionary
Orson Wells — *John Alden, Francis Cooke, and Richard Warren*
stage & film actor, director, producer
Humphrey Bogart — *John Howland*
film actor

John Clarke
Mayflower pilot

John Clarke had made several trips to Jamestown, Virginia, as well as to New England prior to piloting the *Mayflower* to Plymouth. John Clarke is mentioned in a letter written by Robert Cushman on June 11, 1620.

"We have hired another pilot here, one Mr. Clarke, who went last year to Virginia with a ship of kine."

This 1619 trip to Virginia was with Captain Thomas Jones of the *Falcon*, a some-time pirate.

Pilgrim Eating Customs

Pilgrims used a knife, spoon, a large napkin, and fingers...no forks when they ate. They also shared plates and drinking vessels. It was the custom in a Pilgrim household for adults to be served dinner by the children who would eat after the adults whatever food remained.

Smallpox

Some stones reveal disasters that befell more than the individuals named on the stone. This Gravestone only hints at the disastrous smallpox epidemic that engulfed the American colonies during the period from 1765 through 1777.

Zenas Rider 1766
Bethia Rider 1766

Here Lies buried
Mr Zenas Rider who
Dec'd Jan'ry 1766
With the Smallpox in ye 41st year of
his Age Also Bethia Sister to
above Named Dec'd the same
time in her 39th year

"More to dread...than from the Sword of the Enemy"
George Washington

In the early years of the American Revolution, in addition to shortages of men and supplies, George Washington faced an invisible killer he had once battled as a teenager. Where the earlier fight had threatened only his life, at stake in this confrontation were thousands of lives, both military and civilian alike, the continued viability of Washington's army, and the success of the war being waged for independence from Britain. The unseen killer, caused by a highly contagious virus, was smallpox, which Washington described in 1777 as potentially a greater threat "than the Sword of the Enemy."

Excerpted from the Mount Vernon Annual Report

William Drew Tufts

Was he killed by Pirates?

In memory of

William Drew Tufts
Son of Jona & Priscilla Tufts,
Born Nov. 9 1797
Died at the Island of Cuba
March 29 1816
aged Nineteen years.

Green as the bay tree, ever green,
With its new foliage on,
The young, the healthful have I
seen,
I pass'd, and they were gone.

The period between 1814 and 1825 was a bloody time for American marine interests in the Caribbean with repeated battles between American ships and ferocious pirates. There were three thousand pirate attacks on merchantmen between 1815 and 1823 on and around Cuba.

One can not find direct evidence as to the cause of young William's death but it is probably safe to assume that he was aboard one of the Plymouth ships that were attacked off Cuba by blood thirsty pirates.

The first governor of Plymouth Colony was John Carver, who was elected in November 1620, while aboard the Mayflower. He was again elected in March 1621. He died in April 1621

Joseph Churchill

Both Father and Son Lost at Sea

Erected
in memory of
Joseph Churchill,
died at sea. Nov. 1836
aged 54 years
Sailed from Boston in the Brig Plymouth Rock,
bound for Rochelle in France
and supposed foundered at sea.
Also his children:
Joseph Lewis, died at sea 1842 on board
the Brig Androscoggin of Portland
Marcia Goodwin died May 2, 1829, aged 22 years

Stone Tops

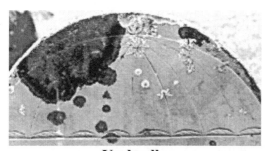

Umbrella

Winged head

Winged head with scallop collar

Portrait style

Stone Top Carvings

Skull and Crossed Bones

Ship Mayflower on Howland stone

Weeping Willow

Crossed Bones and Two Angels

Coll Isaac Lothrop

This Stone is
erected to the memory of
that unbiased judge
Faithful Officer, sincere
Friend and honest Man
Coll Isaac Lothrop
who resigned this Life
on the 26th day of April
1750
in the 43 year of his age.

*Had Virtues Charms the power to
save
Its faithful Votaries from the
grave
This stone would neer possess the
fame
Of being marked by Lothrop's
name.*

Isaac Lothrop was a member of Plymouth's Committee of Correspondence and was elected to the Massachusetts Provincial Congress.

*The first Pilgrims to be married in New England
were Edward Winslow and Susanna White,
both widowed during the first winter.
They were married on May 12, 1621.*

91

William Ring

His grandfather missed the boat

Here lyes ye body of
William Ring
who decd sum time
in April 1729
in ye 77th year of his age.

This William Ring is the grandson of William and Mary Ring who, in 1620, were aboard the Mayflower's companion ship Speedwell. The Speedwell had to turn back because of dangerous leaking

According to Capt. John Smith, writing in 1622,

> 'They left the coast of England the 23 of August, with about 120 persons, but the next day the lesser ship sprung a leake, that forced their return to Plimoth, where discharging her and 20 passengers, with the great ship and a hundred persons besides sailers, they set saile againe the Sixt of September.'

Among the twenty who stayed behind were Robert Cushman, one of the Separatist leaders, and William Ring, of the Leiden congregation. Cushman wrote of the short but frightful voyage aboard the Speedwell, 'Poore William Ring and my selfe doe strive who shall be meate first for the fishes.'"

Joseph Bartlett

Is this epitaph predicting messages from the grave?

Here lyeth buried ye body of
Joseph Bartlett
who departed this life April
ye 9th 1703 in ye
38th year of his age
J. B.
*Thousands of years after
blest Abell's fall Twas said of
him being dead he speakth yet
From silent grave methinks 1
hear a call
Pray fellow-mortall, don't
your death forget You that
your eyes cast on this grave
Know you a dying time must
have.*

Serg. Joseph Bartlett was Born in 1665 at Plymouth and he married Lydia Griswold. Together they had five children none of which was named Abell. Abell is both a first and last name and none of his daughters married an Abell nor were any of his grand children named Abell.

The Pilgrims didn't use forks. They used a knife, a spoon, a large napkin and fingers, and shared plates and drinking vessels.

Revd. Chandler Robbins D D

There were NO PILGRIMS at the first Thanksgiving!

This Stone Consecrated to the memory
Of the Revd Chandler Robbins D D
was erected By the inhabitants of the
first Religious Society in Plymouth
As their last grateful tribute of
respect
For his eminent labors In the ministry
of JESUS CHRIST
Which commenced January 30th 1760
And continued till his death June 30th
1799 Ætatis 61 When he entered
into the everlasting rest
Prepared for the faithful ambassadors
Of the most high God.

*Ah come heaven's radiant Offspring
hither throng
Behold your prophet your Elijah tied
Let sacred symphony attune each
tongue
To chant hosannahs with the virtuous
dead.*

It was not until 1793, 175 years after the Colonists landed, that the name "Pilgrims" was applied to the colonists. In that year, on the celebration of "Forefathers Day" at Plymouth, the Reverend Chandler Robbins, who preached the sermon, used the term. In the sermon, Robbins read a letter written by William Bradford. Bradford's letter described how 101 passengers mustered up the courage to board the Mayflower and begin a treacherous three month voyage to a virtually unknown land. Bradford commented, "They knew they were pilgrims and looked not much on those things, but lifted up their eyes to the heavens, their dearest country, and quieted their spirits." Based on this, Pr. Robbins started calling this band of pioneers, Pilgrims. The name stuck.

Pilgrim Promoter

Alfred Stevens Burbank

Pilgrims to Sunday worship

Speak for yourself John Alden

Two well known pictures commissioned by A S Burbank

A. S. Burbank was a most prolific marketer of local pictures and souvenirs of Plymouth, Mass. He was sixteen when he opened his Pilgrim Bookshop at 6 Main St in the Odd Fellow's Block in 1872. He operated the business and commissioned Pilgrim souvenirs and Plymouth pictures until his retirement in 1932. No one was more indefatigable in presenting the story of the Pilgrims and its imagery to the American public through books, cards, figurines, dishes and other objects.

In 1902 he published and copyrighted "Handbook of Old Burial Hill - Plymouth, MA: Its History, Its Famous Dead, and Its Quaint Epitaphs". More than 100 years later another Burbank and distant cousin pens an update of his out of print work.

95

Name Index and Section Indicator for Old Burial Hill

ALBERSON
Jacob - K
Jacob Warren - K
Josh Warren - K
Lydia - K

ALEXANDER
Charles - P
Charlotte S - P
Deborah – P
Fanny – P
George – P
Georgeianna - P
Georgeiana – P
John – P
John K – P
Samuel – P
Silvanius – P
Sophronia – P

ALLEN
Charles B – P
Elizabeth E – L
Ezra – B
James – H, L
Mary – B
Mary A B – P
Susan H – A

ALLERTON
Issac – O
Mary – O

ATHERTON
Charles Thomas – A
James M – A
Phebe – A

ATTWOOD/
ATWOOD
Abby Jane – K
Darius – L
Elizabeth – L
Experience - B

ATTWOOD/
ATWOOD cont'd
George Hebert – K
Georgie – K
Hannah – B
Henry R – B
Infant – L
Isaac R – B
Joanna – B
John – B
John. Deacon – B, C-W, D
John B – C-E
Lydia – C-W
Martha B – C-E
Mehetabel – L
Sarah – B
Sarah J – K
Sarah, Jane – K
Susanna – L
Temperance – B
Thomas – L
Thomas, Capt – L
Twin daughters – L
Wait – L
William – B
William, Capt – K
William, Jr. – B
William, Perley – K
Willie – K

BACON
Abigail – B
Betsey – B
Charles Henry – B
David – B
David, Esq – B
Elizabeth – B
George – B
Geo., Capt – B
George, Capt – B
George T., 2nd – B
George T., 3rd - B
Henry Sampson – B
Jacob, Rev. – B

BACON continued
Mary – B
Mary T. – B
Nathan – B
Nathan, Capt – B
Rebecca, B
Thomas – B

BAGNALL/
BAGNELL
Benj. – A
Benjamin – A
Bethiah - A
Betsey Crocker – A
Elizabeth – A
Elizabeth S. - A
Lois – A
Lucy – A
Lucy Family – A
Lydia – L
Minerva – A
Richard – A, L
Richard, Capt – L
Sam'l W. – A
Samuel W. – A
Samuel West - A
Sarah F - A

BALL
Albert – L
Lucy - L

BALLARD
Samuel D. – K

BANKS
Mary C. - L

BARDAN
Gershom – N
Mary - N

BARLOW
John – P
John B – P
John W. – P
Mary - P

BARNS/BARNES
Ann Elizabeth – C-E
Ann Frances – C-E
Anson L. – F
Benjamin – N, B
Benjamin, Jr. – M
Betsey G. Ellis – O
Betsey Thomas – A
Betsey Winslow – A
Calvin Carver – N
Charles Elkanah – P
Charlott – B
Corban – B
Corban, Capt. A, B
Corbin, Capt. – B
Eleanor – N
Elenor – N
Ellis – A, D, C-E
Elizabeth – D, C-E
Elizabeth Ishmael – P
Hannah – N, O
Harriet G. – D
Harriet M. –D
Isaac Jr. – A
Jane – A
John – B
Jonathan – B
Joseph – A, B, N
Joseph Jr. – A
Levonzo D. – D, B
Little Lizzie – C-E
Little Willie – C-E
Lizzie – C-E
Mary – A, B, K
Mary A. N. – A
Mary W. – A
Mercy - N
Nancy C. – A
Nathaniel - B, N, O

BARNS/BARNES
Continued
Nathl Jr. – O
Phebe – B
Phebe J. – C-E
Polly – A
Rebecca – M
Rebeckah – M
Rebekak – B, M
Roselia L. – A
Sally – C-E
Samuel – N
Sarah – B, N
Seath – B
Seth – B
Susan L. – F
Will – C-E
William – C-E, N
William, Capt. – C-E
William B – D
William E. – D
William T. – C-E
Willie – C-E
Willie H. -- C-E
Winslow – A
Winslow C. – C-E
Wm – C-E, N
Wm B. – D
Wm Brewster – D
Z., Capt. - A
Zeacheus – A
Zeacheous, Capt. – A

BARRY
Hattie S. – A
Maria – A
Timothy – A
Timothy Jr. – A

BARSTOW
Ichabod W. – C-E
Sarah R. – C-E

BARTLET/
BARTLETT
Andrew, Capt. – B
Angeline – A
Anna M. – D
Ansel – A
Augustus – C-E
Benjamin – C-E, D, G
Benjamin W. – F
Betsy – G
Betsy L. – O
Caleb – F
Caroline – B
Catherine – F
Charles – A
Charles T. – B
Charlotte C. – C-E
Clarrisa – M
Cynthia – B
David – F
Dolly – B
Dorothy – B
Eleazor S. – G
Elisabeth – B
Eliza Ann – B
Elizabeth – B, G, K
Elizabeth Thatcher – B
Elizath – G
Elizth – G
Elkanah – B
Ephraim – F
Experience – A
Fear – F
Five Children - G
Four children – A
Frederick – K
Hannah – A, D, F, G
Hannah S. – B
Hariot – B
Henry – M
Infant – F
Isaac – F
Isaac, Capt. – F
James – B

97

BARTLET/
BARTLETT
Continued
James, Capt. – B
James, Jr. – B
James T. – B
James Thomas – B
Jamima – D
Jane – B
Jane Sampson – B
Jenny – G
Jerusa – G
Jesse – O
John – B, C, D, F G
John, 3rd – B
John Lewis – B
Joseph – C-E, D, F, K
Joseph, Capt. – C-E
Lemuel – G
Lewis – B
Lothrop – G, K
Lucia – A
Lucy D. – C-E
Lydia – G
Margaret – G
Margaret, J. – L
Margaret James – L
Margtt – G
Martha – O
Mary – B, K, L
Mary A. – B
Mary Ann – L
Mary T. – B
Mercy – B
Nathaniel – A, B, L
Phebe – C, N
Polly – A, B, F
Rebecca – C-E, F
Rebecca A.- A, B
Rebecca T. – B
Rebeckah T. – B
Rebekah – D
Robert – F, G
Ruth - M
Samuel – C- E, G, K

BARTLET/
BARTLETT
Continued
Samuel, Esq. – G, K
Samuel, Lt. – K
Samuel, Esqr. – G
Sarah – B, F,G, L
Sarah Taylor – L
Silvanus, T. – B
Solomon – L
Sophia – K
Sylvanus – O
Sylvanus, Taylor – B
Stephen – A, B
Susan – B, C-E
Susan T – B
Susan Thatcher – B
Thomas – B, G, L, M
Thomas, Capt – L
Thomas, 2nd – N
Truman – A
William – B, C, L
William, Capt – L
William Thos. – L
Zacheus, Dr. – D

BARTRETT
Benjamin W. – F
Catherine – F

BASSETT
Abbie – B
Thomas – B

BATES
Abby Washburn – B
Abigail H. – P
Benj. – F, O
Benjamin F. – F, O
David – F
Ebenezer P. – A
Emily F. – B
Hira – A
John – A
John B., Col – B

BATES cont.
Martha – A, O
Mary – B
Ozin – P
Thankful – F

BATTLES
Angline - J
Bradford, L. – J
Clarisa – J
Deborah – B
Elizabeth – B
Jane W. – J
Jane Wight – J
John – B, J
Lydia – B
Nancy – J
Nancy H. – J
Rebecca – J
Samuel – B
William – B

BAXTER
Abner Morton – G
Ann Elizabeth – G
Charles Homer – G
James – G

BENSON
Charles A. – A
Martin – A
Martin L. – A
Phebe – A

BISHOP
Abigail – F, C-E, F
Catharine B. – F
George – F
Henry – F
John – F
John, Capt. – F
John Jr., Capt. – F
John Dea – F
Katie B – F
Mary – F

BISHOP continued
Sarah T. – F
William – F

BLACHOWICZ
James – B, D, K

BOSWORTH
Hannah Howland – H

BOURASSO
Hannah – F

**BOUTELL/
BOUTELLE**
Ann Goodwin – D
Ann L. – D
Caleb, Dr. – D
Ellen G. – D
Nathl G – D

**BOWEN/BOWRIN/
BOWRN**
Mary – M

BOYSE
Elener, see PRATT

BRADFORD
Alice – B
Amos – K
Andrew J. – F
Anna – K
Bathsheba – C-W
Betsy – F
Charles – C-W
Consider – B
Cornelius – B
David – F
David, Capt. – F
David L. – F
Desire H. – F
Ebenezer N. – C-W
Ebenezer Nelson – C-W
Eleanor – B

BRADFORD continued
Eleanor Morton – B
Elizabeth – B, K
Elsey – K
Ephraim – B
Hannah – B
Hannah E. – C-W
Isaac – K
James – B, K
Joan – D
John H. – B
Joseph – B
LeBaron – K
Lemuel – B, C-W
Lemuel, Capt. – B
Lydia – B
Lydia H – F
Lydia Nelson – C-W
Mary – B, C-W
Mary B. – K
Nancy – K
Nathaniel – B
Pelham – J
Rebecca – B
Ruth – K
Sally – B
Sally H. – C-E
Sarah – B, K
Selah – J
Susan – G
Thomas – C-W
William – B, K
William, Esq, Gov – B
William [Gov} – B
William, Hon. Maj. – B
Zephaniah – C-E

BRAMHALL
Benj. Jr. – L
Benjamin – L
George – B
Grace – L
Joseph – L
Joseph, Capt – K
Joshua – K, L

**BRAMHALL
continued**
Lucy – B
Lucy – B
Marcy Warren – L
Martha – K
Mary – K, L
Mary Bennet – L
Mercy – K
Phebe J. – L
Priscilla – L
Remember – L
Sarah – K
Silvanus – K

BRECK
Mary – C-E
Moses – C-E
Sarah Taylor – C-E

BREWSTER
Child – E
Ellis, Capt. – E
Elizabeth – E
Elizabeth T. – E
Elizabeth Taylor – E
Nancy – E
William – E
William, Capt. - E

BRIGHAM
Antipas – B
Mercy – B
Mercy M – B
Mercy Sampson – B

BROOKS
Betsy – B
Samuel – B

BROWN
Abigail Allen – B
Alice A. - B
Alice Rice – C-E
Ann – C-E

99

BROWN continued
Ann A Neal – B
Bambas A. – B
Charles – K, P
Charles S. – P
Charlotte Ann – P
Lemuel – C-E
Lucy Cotton Jackson – K
Lydia – B
Lydia Allen – B
Lydia Howland – H
Margaret – B
Margret – B
Martha – B
Mary – B
Mary Sophia – K
Nabby B
Priscilla – B
Robert – B
Robert, Esq. B
Samuel – B
Sarah – C-E
Sarah Palmer – C-E
William – B
William, Esq. – B

BRUNT
Bessie – B

BRYANT
Homer – A

BUGBEE
Aurin, Rev. – B
Deborah B Gooding – B
James H., Rev. – K

BULLARD
Benjamin – B
Benjamin Dexter – B
Emily – F, P
Mary – B

BURBANK
Amy Allen – N
Betsey – N
Daniel Torrey – N
Ezra – N
Hannah – N
John – N
John, Jr. – N
Lucy – N
Lydia – N
Mercy – N
Nehemiah – N
Polly – N
Timothy – N

BURGESS/BURGIS
BURGISS
America, Capt – F
Fenelon, T – A
Four Infants – B
George Augustus – B
Georgina – A
Hannah Ellis – B
James W – B
Jane – A
Jane F – B
John Jr., Capt – A
Joseph – A
Joseph w. – B
Lucy – F
Nathaniel – A
Sally – A
Sarah F
Simon R – B
Susannar – A
Thomas – A

BURN/BURNS
Catherine – L
Elizth – B
Ellen – L
James L
James H - L

BURN/BURNS
Continued
Jonathan – B
Mary – L
Mitchell – B
Rose – L
Samuel – B

BURT
Edward – B
Elizabeth –B
Hannah F
Laban – F
Thomas B – B

BUTLER
Alma May – C-E
John S. – C-E
Mary D. – C-E

CALDWELL
Martha T. – D

CALLAHAN
Marge – K

CALLAWAY
George W. – L
Mary Ann – L

CARVER
A daughter – B
Abbigail – N
Betsey – A
Dorothy – B
Eliza – N
James – B
Joanna – A, N
Joseph – B
Josiah – B
Josiah, Capt. – N
Josiah, Dea – B
Mary - A

100

CARVER continued
Nancy – A, N
Nathaniel, Capt. – A, N
Nathaniel, Jr. – A
Sarah – A
Stephen A, N
Theodore S. N

CASSADY
Ann – L
John – L

CASWELL
Caroline – N
Daniel – N
Harvy – N

Henry N

CHANDLER
Hannah – G, K
Hannah – B, G
John B. – G
John T. – G
Lucy S. G
Reuben, Capt. – K

CHASE
Abigail – N
George E. – N
Henry – N
John – N
Mary Deacon – D
Samuel R. – N
William – N

CHIPMAN
Hope Howland – H

CHURCH
Joseph – H

CHURCHALL/
CHURCHELL/
CHURCHILL
A son – B
A daughter – B
Abigail – B
Abigail Worcester – B
Abigail – A, B
Abigail H. – P
Adrianna – B
Alice G. - K
Almira H. – F
Amelia – C-W
An Infant – N
Annie G. – K
Ansell – B

Asenath – B
Barnabas – A
Benjamin – N
Bethiah – B
Betsey – K
Catharine Bridgham – A
Charles – A
Charles O. – K
Charles Thomas – C-W
Child – C-E
Daniel – B
David – A, B
Edward – C-W
Eleazor – B
_lenor – B
Elizabeth – A, B
Elizabeth C. – P
Elizabeth H, - P
Elkanah – B
Ephraim – B
Esther – N
Eunice – B, C
Experience – B
Ezra – C-W
George – C-W
Hannah – A, B
Hannah T. – A
Heman – B, F

CHURCHALL/
CHURCHELL/
CHURCHILL
Continued
Isaac – B
Jane – B
Lennie E. – K
Jesse – B
Jesse, Capt. – B
Job – A, K
John – B, F
Joseph – C-W
Joseph, Capt. – C-W
Joseph Lewis – C-W
Lewis – A
Lucretia A. Bacon – K
Lucy – A, B
Lydia A, B
Lydia A. – B
Lydia L. – C-W
Marcia Goodwin – C-W
Mary – A, B
Mary A. – B
Mary Elizabeth – A
Mercy – C-W
Nancy – A, B
Nathaniel – B
Olive – F
Otis – N
Priscilla – B
Rebecca – B
Rebecca T. – A
Rebeckah – B
Rufus – C-E
Ruth – N
Sally – A, B
Samuel – B
Sarah – A, B
Seth – A
Silvanus – P
Solomon, Dea. – B
Stephen – A, B
Stephen, Capt. – B
Susan – N

101

CHURCHALL/
CHURCHELL/
CHURCHILL
Continued
Susan E. – C-W
Sylvanis H. – K
Thaddeus, Lt. – B
Thomas – A
Timoth – G, K
Twins – P
William – B
William C. – P
Wilson – N
Zacheus – B

Clark/Clarke
Abigail – C-W, F
Alice Hallett Nichols – K
Andrew – K
Elizabeth – B
Eliza H. – C-E
Ella Marie – C-W
Hannah – K
James – K
John – C-E, K
John, Capt. – C-W
John, 3rd – C-W
John T. – C-W
Mary – C-E, I
Mary Roberts – C-E
Nathaniel – F, K
Nathaniel, Esq. – K
Rebecca M. – C-W
Rebecca Thomas – C-W
Sally C. – N
Samuel – I
Sarah R. – C-E
Susanna – K
Thomas – K
William. – K
Zoeth – C-W
Zoheth – C-W

COAL
Isaac – F
Sarah – F

COB/COBB
A daughter – D
Alice E. – K
Cornelius – O
Ebenezer – N
Elizabeth – C-W, O
Ephraim – F
Eugene H. – K
Francis – C-W
Grace – O
Haddie H. – K
Harriet – K
Isaac E. – O
Isaac Eames – O
Job – O
John – D, N
John K. – B, K, M
Josiah – D
Laura L. – K
Lazarus, Capt. – F
Lemuel – F, K
Margaret – F
Mercy – N
Mary – D
Patience – O
Ruth – O
Sarah – D
Susanna – M
William, Esq. – C-W

COLBY
Eliza – C-E
Elizabeth – C-E
Joshua – C-E

COLE
Caroline E. – B
Cyrus – G
Deborah B. – B
Ephraim – B
James - B

COLE continued
Jane R. – B
Rebecca - B
Rebecca Gray – B
Sally – B
Samuel – B
Sarah – B
Susan – G
Timothy, Rev. – G

COLGAN
Ann – L
John – L
Thomas – L

COLLIER
Ezra – J
Mary Atwood – J
Mary S. – J

COLLINGWOOD
Eleanor – C-E
John – C-E
John B., Lt. – C-E
Joseph, Capt. – C-E
Joseph W., Capt. – C-E
M. A. – C-E
Martha T. – C-E
Mary – C-E
Nellie F. – C-E
Rebecca W. – C-E
Robert S. – C-E
Susan – C-E
Thomas – C-E
Thomas, Corp. – C-E
William – C-E
William, Jr. – C-E
Willie B. – C-E
Willie L. – C-E

COLLINGS
Gamalie, Capt. – L
Infant – L
Lois – L

COLLINS
James – L
James, Capt. – L
Lois – L
Mary – L

COOK/COOKE
Caleb – L
Marcy – M

COOPER
Emeline P. – B
Esther – B
George – B, C-E
George W. – C-E
Hannah – B
Jerusha – B
John – B
Joseph – B
Joseph, Capt. – B
Joseph, Jr. – N
Joseph, Jr., Capt. – N
Lucy – B
Lucy T. – B
Lucy Taylor – B
Mary – C-E
Mary B. – B
Mary C. – C-E
Richard, Capt. – B
Richard – B
Sylvia – N
William – B

CORNISH
David, Capt. – B
Mary – B
Mary Z. – K
Mary Zorda – K
Mercy – B
T. E. Capt. – K
Thomas – K
Thomas E., Capt. – K
Zoraday – K
Zoraday T. – K

COTTON
Anonymous – J
David Barnes – K
Edward – J
Hannah – J, K
Joanna – K
John – J
John, Esq. – K
Josiah – J, K
Josiah, Capt. – B
Josiah, Esq. – K, J
Josiah, Hon., Esq. – J
Lydia – B, K
Martha – K
Mary – K
Priscilla – K
Rachel – K
Roland – J
Rosseter – K
Rosseter, Dr. – K
Rosseter, Esq. K
Rossiter – K
Rossiter M. – K
Samuel A. – J
Sarah D. – B
Seven sons of Josiah – J
Son of John – J
Temperance – B
Theophilus, Col. – K
Theophilus, Col., Esq. – K
Thomas, Capt. – K
Thomas Smith – K
Ward, Rev – J
William C. – K

COURTIES
Elisabeth – B
Fraincis, Jr. – B

COVENTON
Elizabeth – C-E
Elizabeth Hueston – C-E
Thomas – C-E

COVINGTON
Mary – N
Sarah – N
Thomas, Capt. – N

COWEN
Ann – B
Ann T. – B
Mary Ann – B
Robert – B
Robert, Capt. – B

COX
Elias – B, F
Elias E. – F
Eliza – F
Eliza O. – F
James – B
Nancy Holmes – B
Patience – B

CRAIG
David – C-E
David N. – C-E
Mary Ann – C-E

CRANDON
Benjamin – F
Benjamin, Esq. – F
Jane – F
Mary B. – F
Nancy B. – F
Ruth – F
Sarah – F
Sukey – F

CROADE
Deborah – M
John – M

103

CROMBIE/
CROOMBIE?
CRUMBIE
Calvin – K
Deborah – K
Fanney – K
James – K
Kimball – K
Naomi – K
William – K
William, Capt, - K
William, Dea. – K
Zerviah – K

CROSWELL
Andrew – B
Andrew, Esq. – B
David – B
Joseph – B
Joseph Jr. – B
Lucy – B
Mary – B
Rebecca – B
Sarah – B

CROWE
William – G

CURRIER
Daniel – C-W
Ezra – C-W
Freddie – C-W
Susan E. – C-W
Winnie S. – C-W

CURTIS
Caleb – F
Ebenezer – B
James – B
Jonathan – B
Lydia – N
Marye – B
Nathaniel – N
Sallie – B
Zacheus – N

CUSHING
Nathan, C. – A

CUSHMAN
Mary - O
Robert – O
Ruling Elder – O
Thomas, Elder – O

DARLING
Jonathan – K
Martha – K

DAVEA/DAVEE/
DAVIE
Betsey – N
Deborah – N
Deborah C. – A
Ebenezer – A
Ebenr – A
Elizabeth – N
Esther – N
Fanny Eddy –N
George – A
Harriot – N
Harriot E. – N
Ichabod – N
Ichabod, Capt – N
Isaac – C-E
Jane – N
Jedidah – N
Jerusha – N
Joanna _ N
John – A
John L. – A
Nancy – N
Nathaniel C. – A
Priscilla A, N
Rhoda C. – C-E
Robart – N
Robart, Capt – N
Robert – N
Robert, Capt. – N
Sarah – N
Sarah J. – N

DAVEA/DAVEE/
DAVIE
Soloman, Capt. - N
Soloman, Jr. – N
Thomas – N

DAVIS
A son – K
Anne E. – N
Betsey B. – N
Eliza – C-E
John R. – N
Joseph – C-E
Frances Marion – B
Mercy – K
N. M. – B
Rebecca – K
Samuel –K
Thomas – K
Thomas, Capt. – K
Tomb – A
Wendall, Hon. – K
William – K
William, Hon. – K
Winslow M. – N

DEACON
Daniel – D
James – D
Mary – D
Polly T. D
Susan A. – D

DELANO/DELENO
A daughter – K
Abigail – N
Bathsheba –N
Henrey – K
Judah – K
Lydia – A
Nathan – N
Nathan, Capt. – N
Penelope - K
Sarah – N
Sarah J. - N

104

DELANO/DELENO
Salome – K
Sarah – D

DELEANY
Dennis – L
Sarah – L

DICKENSON
Elizabeth Howland – H

DICKSON
John – B
Mary – B
Phebe – B
S. R. – C-E
Samuel – B
Samuel R. – C-E
R. F. – C-E
Ruby F. C-E

**DIER/DYAR/
DYRE/DYER**
Bethia – K
Charles – K
Charles, Capt. – K
Hannah – B, J
John – B
John, Capt. – B
Mary – K
William, Capt. – J

DIKE/DYKE
Anthony, Capt. – F
J. Russell – C-E
Mary – A
Molley – F
Parney Young – A
Phebe Soule – C-E
Rebecah – A
Russell, R – C-E
Simeon – A
Thomas – F
William, P. G. – A

DILLARD
Benjamin – N
Mercy – N
Nancy – N
Polly – N

DIMAN
Abigail B. – B
Abigail N. – B
Benjamin – B
Daniel – B
David – B
Elizabeth – B, C
Elezebeth – B
Erastus W. – B
Ezra S. – B
Hannah – O
Hattie A. – B
Jonathan, Dea – O
Josiah – B
Josiah Dea – B
Judith Gray – B
Lizzie G. – B
Lois – B
Maria S. – B
Mary – B
Mary N. – B
Miriam G. – B
Polly – F
Sarah N. – B
Sophia – B
Susanna – B

DITMAN
Valentine – B

DOANE
Mary – M

DOGGET/DOGGETT
Ebenezar – F
Elizabeth – F
Jane - F
Seth – F

DOTEN
Abby Davee – L
Abigail – B
Bathsheba James –F
Betsey P. – C-W
Charles A. – C-W
Daniel – N
Ebenezer – C-W
Edward – C-E, C-W
Elizabeth – N
Esther – C-W
Eunice – C-W
4 infant daughters –F
Hannah – F
Hellen – C-W
Isaac – F
Jabez – F
Jain – G
James – F, L
James, Capt. – N
James, Jr. – N
Jerusha – B
John – F
Joseph – N
Joseph, Capt – F, N
Lewis – C-W
Louisa S. – C-W
Lydia – L
Martha – F
Martha Torrey – F
Mary – F, N
Mary W. – C-E
Mercy – N
Nathaniel – N
Polly – F
Prince – N
Salina – C-W
Sally F, N
Samuel – C-W, N
Samuel H. – L
Slyvanus H. – N
Susan – N
Thomas – F
Thomas, Capt. – B
William – B, F, G

DOTEY
Ancel – C-W
Eunice – C-W
Samuel – C-W

DOTY
Elizabeth – K
Joanna – F
Nathaniel – F
Thomas, Capt – K
Thomas, Col. – B, K
Ruth – B

DREW
Abbot – K
Abigail – B
Abijah – L
Addie – K
Ann – B
Ann R. – F
Atwood, Capt. – B
Bathsheba – N
Benjamin – K
Benjamin, Jr. – K
Benjamin, 3rd – K
Betsy – K
Betsy Churchill – K
Charity S – B
Charlotte A. – K
David – B, C-E
Deborah – K
Desire – K
Ebenezer – K
Eliza – B
Eliza A. – B
Elizabeth – B, K
George H. – B
Hannah – B
Helen Augusta – B
Isaac – K
James – B
James H. – A
John – F
John C. – B
Joseph – K

DREW
Leman L. – B
Lemuel – B, K, L
Lemuel, Dea – K
Lucinda – B
Lucy – L
Lydia – B
Lydia W. – B
Lydia Williams – B
Malachi – K
Margaret – P
Mary – B
Nicholas – B
Nicholas H. – K
Nicolas – N
Priscilla – B
Priscilla Washburn – G
Rebekah – B
Sally – B, C-E, L
Sally F. – L
Sarah – C-E, K
Simeone – K
Sophia – K
Sophia B. K
Solomon – B
Solomon A. – B
Stephen – B
Susan H Allen – A
William – B, G
William 2nd – B, G
William R. – B

DUNBAR
John D., Esq. – K
Nancy – K

DUNHAM
Abigail – F
Abigail Thomas – F
Abraham – B
Abraham T. – B
Alice – B
Benjamin – B
Benjamin – F
Betsy – B

DUNHAM
Charley – L
Elijah – B
Elisha – B
Elizabeth – F
Elizabeth C. – B
Eunice – B
George – F
George, Capt. – F
Isaac – B
J. A. – L
Mary – N
N. E. – L
Nancy – F
Patience – B
Robert – A
Sally – A
Silvanus – N
Susan Mason – B
William – F

DURFY/DURPHEY
Marey – B
Mary – B
Peleg – B

EDDY
Ann Eliza – K
Ann Elizabeth – K
Betsey – K
Frances M. – B
George – K
Henry F. – F
John – K
Seth W. – B
Willie O. – B

EDWARD
John – L
Lydia – L
Polly – L

ELLIOT/ELLIOTT
Clarrisa – G
Daniel R., Esqr. - B

106

ELLIOT/ELLIOTT
Infant son – G
Mercy G. – G
Samuel – G
Susan Louisa – B

ELLIS
Betsy – B
Betsy G. – O
George S., 2nd – B
Helena C. – B
Jane – N
Jenne – N
Lydia W. – N
Mary H. – B
Nathaniel – N
Nathaniel, Capt. – N
Rebecca – N
Samuel – N
Stevens – B
William – B

ERLAND
Edwin F. – O
Henry – O
Martha A. – O
Sally C. – O

FARMER
Phebe – F
Thomas, Capt. – F

FARRELL
Andrew – L

FAUNCE
Abigail – B
Bamabas, Capt. – B
Caroline A. – L
Charles B. – C-W
Charles L. – M
Elizabeth – B
Hannah – M
James S. – C-W
Jerusha – M

FAUNCE
John – B
John B., Capt. – M
Mary – B, C-W
Nathl – B
Olive – L
Olive Jane – M
Peleg – L
Peleg, Dea. – L
Priscilla – B
Sarah – B
Thaddeus – C-W
Thomas – B
Thomas, Elder – B
William H. – C-W
Zilpah – B

FIELD
Charles – B
E. – A
R. – A

FORSTER/FOSTER
Elisha – B
Eunice – B
Gershem – N
Gershom – B
Hannah – B
Job – B
John – B
John, Dea – N
John, Jr. – N
Lemuel – B
Lois – B
Margaret – B
Mary – B
Mercy – A, B
Nathaniel – A
Nathl – A
Samuel – B
Seth – B
Susanah – A
Thomas – B
Thomas, Esq. – B
Thomas, Jr. – B

FREEMAN
Abner F. – L
Betsey D. – L
E. – G
Elizabeth – G
F. – G
F., Rev. – L
Frederick, Rev. – G
Frederick, Russell – G
Nath'l – l

FRISBEE
Lena Hatch – P

FULGHUM
Joseph – I
Joseph, Capt. – I
Luraina – I

FULLER
Ann R. – F
Darius – N
George F. – F
John – D
Lizzie Abbot – F
Matilda – N
Rebecca – D
Robert D. – F

GALE
Daniel – B
Elizabeth – B
Noah – B
Rebekah – B
Stephen – L

GAMMONS
Benjamin – F
Deborah - F

GARDNER
Ellen – K
Fanny H. – F
Harwood – F
Mary - K

107

GARDNER continued
Mary Ellen – K
Mehetable – F
William L. – K

GAY
Clara E. – P
Edson M. – P
Harriet H. – P
John B. – P
Timothy E. – P

GIBBS
Thomas H. – F

GLEASON
James G. – C-W
Lucy T. – C-W
Phebe – C-W

GODDARD
Abigail Otis – B
Anne E. – N
Benjamin – B, N
Beulh – A
Daniel – A
Daniel, Jr. – A
Grace Hayman – B
Harriet E. – A
John – A
John, Dr. – B

Lemuel S. – A
Lucy – N
Lydia – A
Mary – A, B
Mary Simmons – A
Mercy – A
Polly – A
Rufus – B
Sarah – B
William – B

GOODING
Deborah B. – B

GOODWIN
Abagail T. – N
Abigail, - D
Anna – C-W
Anna Lewis – C-W
Charles – C-E
Charles T. – N
Desire – N
Edward J. – D
Fear – K
H. B. Rev. – B
Hannah – D, K
Hannah J. – K
Heverland T. – N
Isaac – C-E
John – K
Lazarus – D
Lazarus, Esq. – M
Lewis – C-W
Lewis, Capt. – C-W
Lorenzo – C-W
Lucretia Watson – B
Lucy – J
Lydia – D, M
Lydia C. – C-E
Mary Ann – D
Molly – D
Molly I. - D
Nancy – K
Nathaniel – D, M
Nathaniel, Esq. – D

Nathaniel, Gen. – D
Nathl – D
Nathl, Esq. – D
Nathl, Gen – D
Nathaniel – D
Roby – M
Ruth – D
Thomas – D, N
Timothy – J
William – C-E

GORHAM
Desire Howland – H

GOULD
Drusilla – C-E

GRATON
Alwin M. – F
Charles Alwin – F
Mary D. – F

GRAY
Edward – I
Joanna – J
John – J
Mary J

GREEN
Clarisa A. – B
George F. – B
Marcia C. – F
William C. – F

GRIFFIN
Edward P. – C-W
Granvill C. – C-W
Granvill S. – C-W
Granville C. – C-W
Olive W. – B
Rebecca D. – C-W
Rebecca J. – C-W

HALL
Betsey Thomas – C-W

Daniel – N
Eber – C-W
Elizabeth – C-W
Emma Sherman – C-W
Isaac T. – P
Joanna A. – K
John T. – C-W
Lewis – L
Mary – C-W
Mary A. – L
Mary E. – P
Nathan T. – F
Reuben – K

108

HALL continued
Sarah – F

**HAMMATT/
HAMMETT**
Abraham, Capt. – K
A. Capt. – K
Abraham – H
Abraham, Capt. – H
E. P. – H
Esther P. – H
Experience – K
Jabez – K
John Howland – H
Lucy – K
Priscilla – H
Sophia – H
William – H

HARLOW
Albert – L
Albert B. – B
Amaziah – L
Ammaziah – L
Ann – M
Ansel H. – F
Barnabas L. – B
Bathsheba – F
Benjamin – M
Betsey – B, L, M
Betsey J. – B
Caleb Bowtell – B
Catherine – B
Cora E. – K
David – K
Deborah – N
Desiah – L
Desire – L
Eliza S. – K
Elizabeth – L
Elizabeth A. – L
Elizabeth F. – B
Ellis J. – A
Ellis J., Capt. – A
Experience – K

HARLOW continued
Ezra, Capt. – N
George H. – L
Gracy – L
Hannah – B, K, L, N
Henry – L
Horace – K
Ichabod – L
Ivory – N
Ivory L. – K
Ivory Lewis – K
Jabez, Capt. – K
James – O
Jerusha – A
Jesse – L
Jesse, Capt. – L
John – L
John, Capt. – J
John, Jr. – L
John H. – B, L
John W. – M
Josiah – O
Lazarus – L
Lazarus, Capt. – L
Lewis – B
Lewis O. – B
Lot, Dea – M
Lucy – L, N
Lydia – N
Marcy – M
Mary – B, L, M
Mary A. – M
Mary L. – L
Mary Morton – B
Mary L. Finney – B
Mercy – A, O
Nancy – L
Nathaniel – B, M
Noah – L
Patience L, O
Peter A. – B
Pheby Ann – M
Priscilla – F
Rebecca – K, N
Rebecca B. – K

HARLOW continued
Rebecca H. – K
Rebekah – K
Remember – O
Ruth R. – M
Sally – B. L
Samuel – L, O
Samuel, Capt. – O
Sarah – A, L, M, N
Sarah B. – K
Seth – A, F, M
Silvanus – L
Silvanus, Capt. – L
Stephen – B, M
Tho's P. –A
William – J, M, N
William R. – J
William M. – M
Wm., Jr. – B
Zacheus – N
Zephaniah, Capt. – O

HATCH
Isaac, Dr. – P
Lena – P
Phila H. – P

HATHAWAY
Allen – A
Edward – P
Lucy N. Morton – P
Priscilla Whiting – P

HAYDEN
Caroline F. – C-E
Thomas W. – C-E

HAYWARD
Beza, Esq. – B
Beza, Jr. – B
Charles L. – B
Edward – B
Elizabeth Ann – B
Ezperience – B
G. W. – B

109

HAYWARD
continued
J. A. – B
Joanna – B
Mary W. – B
Nathan – B
Nathan, Dr. – B
Penelope P. – B

HEDGE
Abigail – B
Barnabas – B
Barnabas, Capt. – B
Mercy – B
Tomb – A

HEMMERLY
Barbara – B
William – B
William K – B

HICKS
Elizabeth Howland – H

HILL
Andrew – F
Elisabeth – F
Jonathan – B
Mary – B

HOBART
Betsey – B
Ellen – B
Priscilla, Madam – B
Noah, Rev. – B

HODGE/HODGES
Betsey Hayward – B
Michael, Esq. – B
Michael – B

HOLBROOK
Amelia – B
Ann Elisabeth C-E
Bethiah – B

HOLBROOK
continued
Eliphalet – B
Eliphalet, Capt. – B, F
Gideon, Capt. B, C-E
Jeremiah – B, K
Jeremiah, Capt. – B
Lizzie – B
Lucy – B
Mary – F
Noah – B
Peggy – K
Sally – B
Two infants – B

HOLLIS
Abigail – B
Elizabeth Owen – B
Henry – B

HOLMES
Abigail – F
Abigail – F
Abner – D
Adoniram J. – F
Albert, Capt. – C-E
Albert Henry – C-E
Alvan E. – N
Ansel – B
Ansil – B
Antoinette – B
Barnabas – C-W
Bathseheba D. F
Bathsheba James – F
Benjamin – C-W
Benjamin 2nd – B
Bethiah – B
Betsey – N
Betsey C. – C-W
Betsy – A, N
Carrie Clifton – C-E
Catharine – N
Cephas A. – F
Irving B. – K
Jeannette – F

HOLBROOK
continued
Jeremia, Jr. – F
Jerusha T. – C-E
Joanah – D
Joann – K
Joanna – N
John – H, N
John C. – B
Joseph – F, B
Joshua – F
Lemuel D. – C-W
Lewis – N
Lewis, Capt. – N
Lois – H
Louisa – F
Louisa Savery – F
Lucy – N
Lydia – B, F
Lydia M. – B
Marcey – A
Marcy – F, N
Mariah – C-W
Martha – B, F
Mary – D, F
Mary Brewster – D
Mary E. – C-W
Mary S. – F
Mary T. – C-W
Massena Francis – B
Mehitable – A
Mercy – F
Miriam C. – B
Nancy – B, F
Nathan – F, N
Nathaniel – F, N
Nathll – A, F, N
Nathaniel, Jr. – C-W
Patience C. – F
Pella M. – B
Peter B. – F
Phebe – A, N
Polly – A, C-W, F, N
Priscilla – B, O
Rebekah – N, K

HOLBROOK
continued
Richard – F
Richard, Capt. – F
Richard, Jr. – F
Richard, 2nd - - F
Ruth – C-W, F
Ruth G. – C-W
Rufus – B
Samuel A. – A
Samuel B. – B
Samuel N. – C-W
Sarah – F
Sarah M. – A
Susan C. – C-W
Susan W. – A
Truman – F
William – F
William, Capt. – F
William, 3rd – F
William 3rd, Capt. – F
William R. – F
William S. – F
Wm 3rd, Capt. – F
Zephaniah, Capt. B

HOPKINS
Ruth C. – C-W

HOSEA
Daniel – G
Hannah – G

HOVEY
James, Esq. – C-W
Keturah – B
Lydia – C-W
Mary – C-W
Rachael – B
Samuel, Capt. – B

HOWARD
Betiah – A
Ebenezer – A

HOWARD
continued
Hannah – B
James, Capt. – B
James H. – B
John, Capt. – B
John W. – B

HOWES
Ebenezer – G
Hannah – B, G
Jeremiah – B, G
Meriah – G
Moriah – G
Sarah – G

HOWLAND
Caleb – B
Consider – H
Consider – Capt. G
Deborah – B
Desire – H
Elizabeth – H
Emma M. – L
Hannah – H
Isaac, Ens. – H
Jabez, Lt. – H
Jacob – P
Joannah – H
John – J, H
John, Capt. – J
John, Lt. – H
Joseph – G, H
Joseph, Capt – H
Lizzie – P
Lydia – H
Martha – I
Nathl – I
Patience – J
R. M. – L
Rebecca M. – L
Ruth – H
S. S. – L
Sally – P

HOWLAND
continued
Thomas Southworth G
Willie – P
_homas, Cap. – H

HOYT
Betsey – B
Betsey M. – B
Crosby – B
Curtis – P
Curtis F. – P
Harriet – P
Harriet O. – P
Israel – B
Moses – B
Nancy M. – P
Otis – B
Ruth – B

HUESTEN/
HUESTON
Hannah – C-E
Mary – C-E
Nancy Holmes – C-E
Nathaniel – C-E
William – C-E

HUTCHINSON
Adaline – F
Betsey E. – F
Deborah – F
George W. – F
Lob B. – F
Joshua B. – F
Robert, Capt. – F

ISHMAEL
Elizabeth – O

JACKSON
Abraham – B
Andrew – K
Anna – K

111

JACKSON continued
Caroline – M
Charles – K
Comelius – F
Daniel – K
Deborah – D
Desire – B
Edwin – K
Elizabeth – D
Esther – K
Experience – D
Ezra Thayr – D
F. W. – K
Frederic – D
Frederick – D
Frederick Wm – K
Hannah – D, F, K
Harriet – D
Harriet Otis – B
Hezekiah, Capt. – D
Horace – B
Jacob – K
Jeremiah – F
Joann Holmes – K
John T. – K
Lavantia – K
Lideay – K
Lucy – D, K
Lucy Cotton – K
Lydia – K
Marcia – K
Maria T. – K
Mary T. - K
Mercy – D, K
Meriah – K
Meriah M. – K
Nancy B. – F
Nathaniel – B, D
Nath'l – B
Rebecca – K
Ruth – B
Salome – D
Samuel – B, D
Sarah – D, K
Sarah M. – K

JACKSON continued
Sarah May – K
Sophia Gordon – K
Thomas – D, K
Thomas, Capt. – D
Thomas, Esq. – K
Thomas Jr. – K
Thomas T. – K
Thomas 2nd – D
Thomas 3rd – K
William Esq. – K
William Hall – D
Willm – K
Wm – K
Wm, Esq. – K
Wm. Morton – K
Wm R. – K
Woodworth – K

JACOB
John – C-E

JENKS
Cora E. Harlow – K
Fred A. – K
Horace A. – K
Horace B. – K
Lydia A. – K
Fred A. – K
Sonny B. – K

JENNINGS
Joseph – K
Mary – K
One dau – K
Three sons – K

JEWETT
William H. – C-E

JOHNSON
Betsey – F
Betty – B
Danl – B
Daniel Jr. - B

JOHNSON Continued
Joseph – F
Joseph Jr., Capt. – F
Josiah O
Mary C. Banks – L
Patience – O
William A. – L

JONES
Harriett T. – L
Mary – F
Samuel J. – L

JORDAN
James – C-E

JOYCE
Asa – C-W
Lucy A. – C-W

JUDSON
Abigail – G
Abigail Brown – G
Adoniram D. D. – G
Adoniram, Rev. – G
Ann H. – G
Ellen Ypung – G
Elnathan – G
Emily C. – G
Maria E. B. – G
Roger W. – G
Sarah B. – G

KEEN
Lydia – K
Marcy Warren – K
Margaret – K
William – K

KEITH
Betsey M. – B
Lloyd – B

112

KEMPTON

Abigail W. – B
Charles – B
Elizabeth – B
Ephraim – B
John – B
Mary – F
Mother – A
Nathaniel – B
Obed – A
Obed W. – A
Oliver – F
Priscilla – B
Robinson – B
Sally – B, F
Samuel – B
Sarah – B
Woodward – B
Zacheus – B
Zacheus Jr. – B

KENDALL

Elizabeth – G
James, Rev. – G
Lydia – G
Sarah – G

KENDRICK

Albert B. – F
Asa – F
Asa N. – M
Charalotte T. – F
Deborah – F
Eleanor – F
Elenore – F
Elizabeth F. – F
Hattie B. – F
Infant dau. – F
James – F
Mary B. – F
Mary E. – F
Reuben R. – F
Sally K. – F
Sarah V. - M

KENNADY

Esther – L
John – L
Mary Jane – L

KEYES

Lydia – C-E

KIKERT

A. M. E. – L

KING

Harriet A. – N
Isaac B. – N
John – N
John Jr. – N
Nathl – A
Polly – N

KLINGENHAGEN

Anna M. – B
Casper – B
Marie M. – B

LANMAN/LANMON

Almira – p
Ellis T. – C-E
Jane – C-E
John E. – C-E
Mary – F
Peter – F
Samuel – F
Sarah – F

LAPHAM

Elisha – B
Eliza A. – B
Eliza Ann – B
Mary – B

LEACH

Abigail – C-E
Caleb – C-E
David – F
Ebenezer – C-E

LEACH

inney, Capt. – F
Geo. Edwards – F
Louisa – F
Marcia – F
Mercy – F
Rebecca B. – F
Robert Bartlett – F

LEBARON/
LEBARRON

Bartlett – L
Francis – L, M
Frederic – M
Isaac – L, M
Isaac Francis – M
Joseph, Dr. – L
Lazarus, Dr. – H, M
Lidia – M
Lydia – L, M
Margaret – M
Martha Howland – L
Mary Doane – M
Mary Jane – M
Priscilla – H
Sarah – M
William – M
William, Esq. – M

LEMONTE

Abigail – B
Joseph – B
Mathew – B
Marcy – B
Marey – B
Mary – B
Mercy – B

LEBARRON

Abigail – F
Anna – A
Daniel – B
Ephraim Bartlett – F
Mary – B
Nathaniel, Rev. B

113

LEBARRON
continued
Priscilla - B
Rebekah – F
Rev. Mr. – B
Sally – B
Susanna – F
Thos. – B
William – F

LEWIS
Hannah – B
Martha – M
Nathaniel – B
Philip, Capt. – M
Thomas – M
William – E

LINCOLN
Lorrain H. – G
Luke – G
Stella – G

LITTLE
Charles – M
Ephraim, Rev., Mr. – K
Sarah – M
Thomas – M

LOBDELL
Hannah – O
Thomas J. – O

LOTHROP
Ansel, Capt. – K
Bathsheba – M
Benjamin, Capt. – K
David – M
Ellen B
Elizabeth – B, G, K
Experience – K
Freeman – B
Hannah – B
Isaac, Col. – B
Isaac, Esq. – B
Isaac, Hon – B

LOTHROP continued
Isaac, Jr. – B
Joseph – B
Lucy – B
Mary D. – B
Mary W. – B
Melathiah – B
Nathaniel, Dr. – B
Polly – M
Priscilla – B
Thomas, Col – B

LOVELL
Leander – B
Mercy B. – B

LUCAS
Alden – C-W
Catherine – D
Catherine H. – D
Catherine Howland – D
Deborah – C-W
George W. – D
Hannah – D
Hannah – C
Hannah J. – D
Isaac – D
Isaac J. Jr. – D
Lazarus – K
Levi, Capt. – D
Lewis – D
Mary A. – D
Nancy – K
LUCE
Betsey – F
Crosbe – F, L
Crosby – F
Ebenezer – A
Elizabeth – L
Elkanah – L
Sarah – A
Seth – A, F

LUMBER
Elizabeth – C-E
Leuis – C-E
Lewis – C-E

LYNCH
Mehitable P. – F

MAGEE
James, Capt. – L

MANTER
Lucy B. – B
Lucy E. – B
Lucy M. – B
William – B
William F. – B
Winslow – B
Wm. – B

MARCY/MERCY
Abbigail – K
Charles, Capt. – K
Charlott – K
Joseph – K
Lucy – K
Mary – K
Stephen, Dr. – K
Thomas – K

MARSH
Lillis Gill – L
Marcy – L
Thomas – L
Warren – L

MARSHALL
Bartlett – B
Bartlett, Jr. – B
Hannah – B
Ruth – B
Samuel – B

MARSON
Samuel - B

114

MARSTON
Benjamin, Esq. – B
Lucia – B

MATHEWS

Desire – C-E
Mary D. – B
Mary W. – B
Thomas, Capt. – C-E

MAY
Bathsheba – M
Bersheba – M
John – M
Mercy – M
Sarah – M
Thomas – M
William – M

McCARTER
Henry – C-E
Nancy - C-E

McGLATHLIN
Lovica T. – B

McGLAUTHLIN
Priscilla – C-E
Seth – C-E

McLAUTHLIN
Priscilla – C-E
Robert – L

McLEAN
Agnes – B
Richard – B

MENDAL/MENDIL
Jabez – B
Moriah – B

MILLER
Henryetta - B

MITCHELL
Joseph – A
Mary – A

MOORE

Josiah, Rev. – O
Rebecca – O

MOREY
Cornelius – A
Ichabod – F
Mary – F
Mary E. – A
Mary Edwards – A
Polly – A
Susan S. – A
William – A, F
William Thomas – A
Will'm – A

MORRISON
John E. – B
Mercy – B

MORSE
John A. – N
Nancy E. – N

MORTEN/MORTON
Abigail – N
Abraham C. – B
Amasa – B
Anna – O
Barnaba – N
Barnabe – N
Benjamin – N
Betsey – B
Catherine B. – C-E
Dorcas – B
Edward, Capt. – A
Eleanor – A
Eleazar, Capt. – B
Eleazer – B
Elezebeth – B
Elisba – B

MORTEN/MORTON
continued
Elizabeth – B
Elizth – B
Ephraim B

George – B
George, Deacon – B
Hannah – N
Henry – B
Henry Jr. – N
Jacob T. – B
James – B, C
James, 2nd – B
Jane – B
Jemima – B
Jerusha – B
Joanna – B
John – B
John B. – B
John L. – B
Joseph – N, O
Joseph Jr. – O
Josiah, Capt. – B
Lazarus – B
Lemuel – F
Lily – B
Lucis – C-E
Lucy – B
Lucy N. – O
Lydia – B
Lydia T. – N
Marcy – O
Martha – F
Mary – B, F
Mary B. – G, C-E
Mary Edwards – N
Maey Ellen – N
Mary S. – N
Mercy – B
Osborn – A
Nathaniel – B, F
Nath'l, Capt – B
Nathl, 3rd – B
Patience – A
Perez – O

115

MORTEN/MORTON continued
Polly – B
R. H. Herbert – N
Rebecca – B
Rebekah – B
Reliance – B
Ruth – B
Sally – B
Sarah – A, B, F
Seth – B, C-E
Seth, Capt. – B
Silas – B
Susan B. – B
Thomas – B
Timothy – N, O
William – B
William H. – C-E, N
Zephaniah – B
Zepheniah – B

MURDOCK
Elizabeth – K
John – K
John, Esq. – K
Thomas – K

NELSON
Abigail – C-W
Bathsheba – C-W
Charles – C-E
Ebenezer – C-W
Ebenezer, Jr. – C-W
Elisabeth – F
Elisha – C-W
Emilia – G
George – C- W
Hannah – C-W
Lemuel – C-W
Lewis C-W
Lucy – C-W
Lydia – C-W
Martha – C-W
Martha T. – C-W
Mary – C-W

NELSON continued
Ruth – C-W
Samuel Nicols, Capt – F
Sarah W. – G
Stephen S. – G
Thomas – C-W
William – C-W

NICHOLS
Alice Hallett – K
Moses – A
Rizpa – A
Rizpah – A
Susanna – A

NICHOLSON/ NICOLSON
Daniel – M
Elizabeth – M
Hannah – M
Hannah Otis – M
James, Capt. – M
Lucy Mayhew – M
Samuel – M
Sarah – M
Sarah Brinley – M
Thomas, Capt. – M

NICKERSON
Ambrose E. – F
Betsey – F
Betsey Rogers – F
Charles H. – F
Jacob – N
Joan Bradford – F
John – N
John Jr. – N
Lydia – N
Lydia Howland – N
Maria – N
Maria A. – F
Maria H. – F
Mary – F
Mary B. – F
Sophronia Alexander - P

NICKERSON continued
Warren M. – F
William – F
William T. – F
Wm – F

NOONEN
John – K
William – K

NYE
Ann H. – J
Betsey – J
William - J
William C. – J

OLIVER
Elizabeth – B
Peter, Hon., Esq. – B

OSGOOD
John – L

OSMENT
Mary – B

OTIS
Barnabas – F, L
Barnabas Jr – L
Hannah – B, M
Heny – F, L
James – A
John – B, M
Mary – L
Mercy – A
Polly – F, L
Temperance – B

PAINE
Deborah – B
Hannah – M
John S. – B
Mary Brewster – B
Stephen - M

116

PAINE continued

Susan B. – B
Susan W. – B

PALMER
Lewis – B
Nancy K. – B

PATY
Betsey – N
Cordelia – A
Deborah – N
Elizabeth F. – P
Elvira – A
Ephraim – N
Ephraim, Capt. – A
Ephraim, Capt. Jr – P
Geo. Winslow – A
George Winslow – N
Hannah Curtis – A
Jane – A
Jean – A
Jerusha – A
John – N
John, Capt. – N
Lizzie F. – P
Martha – A, N
Meriah – N
Paty Tomb – A
Sarah C. – P
Seth – A
Sylvia – N
Thomas – A
Thomas, Capt. – A
William – B
William A. – P
Wm., Capt. – A

PAULDING
Allie B. – B
Catherine – B
Claribel – B
Eunice – A
Frances A. – B
Hattie E. – B

PAULDING continued
Herbert S. – B
James T. – B
Nancy D. – A
Sylvanus S. – B

PEARSON/PERSONS
Abia – B
B – B
J – B
W – B
William, Capt. – B

PECKHAM
Joseph R. – B
Sarah – B

PERKINS
Betsey – B
Betsey M. – B
Charles T. – B
Elizabeth J. – B
George – B
Hannah – B
James A. – B
Joann – B
Joshua – B
Luke – B
Pella – B
Stephen – B
William – B
William A. – B

PERRY
Adeline F. – F
Caroline – L, P
Charity S. – B
John – C-E
John B. – C-E
John W. – F
L. P. – C-E
Lewis – C-E
Lewis F. – B
Lewis W. – B
Nelson P. – P

PERRY continued
Mary B. – C-E
Rhoda – C-E
Ruth – C-E
Sarah – C-E

PHILLIPS
Cyrus B. – A
Elizabeth – B
Hannah – J
Lucretia – A
Tomson, Capt. J

PIERCE
Abner – A
America – P
Ann Elizabeth – F
Benj. E. – K
Betsey – A
Dorcas Morton – B
Edward F. – K, I, A
Ignatius, Capt. – A
Ignatius Jr. – A
Jean – A
John – A
Lucretia – A
Lucy – A
M. S. – A
Margaret Drew – P
Mary – A
Mary Ann – F
Mary E. – K
Mendal – F
Rebecca Jane – B
Susannah W. – A
Phineas – B
William, Capt. – A
William Nelson – A
Wm., Capt. – 42

PLASKET
Joseph – C-W
Tabitha – C-W

117

POPE
Mary – A
Priscilla – A
Thomas, Capt. – A

PRATT
Elener Boyse – B
Joshua – B
Mary A. – B

PRINCE
Eunice – B
James – B
Thomas Forster – B

PULSIFER/PULSIFOR
Abiel – J
Bethia – J
Bethiah – J
Joseph – J

PURINTON/
PURRINGTON
Jerome W. – B
Lydia – C.
Mary E. – B
William – B

RANDALL
Charles – B
Doughty – K
Elizabeth – K
Enoch – F
George – B
Patience C. B
William – B

RAYMOND/REMOND
Benjamin Gleason – C-E
Betsey – D
Caroline – P
Carolyne – P
Charles – C-E
Ellen – P
Elizabeth – B

RAYMOND/REMOND
continued
Eunice Sturtevant - B
George – C-E
George Jr. – C-E
George LeBaron – C-E
Harvey – F
Harvey H. – F
Henry F. C. – P
Lemuel – D
Lydia – C-E
Lydia A. – C-E
Margaret Hodge – C-E
Mehitable – D
Olive L. – F
Perkins – B
Priscilla – C-E
Samuel B. – P
Samuel E. – P
Samuel Drew – B
William T. – F

REED
Lemuel – E
Lydia – N
Nathan – B, N
Rebecca – B

RICE
Almira J. W. – P
Caroline A. – P
Judson W. – P

RICHMOND
Abbigail – A
Abigail - A
Alpheus – A
Alpheus Jr. – A
Anna – K
Ellen – C-E
Mary B. – K
Saloma – A
Salome – A
Solomon – K
Solomon Hinkley – K

RICHMOND
continued
William – A
William H. – C-E

RICKARD
Adeline W. – F
Anselm – F
Anselm, Capt. – F
A. W. – F
Bathsheba – B
Cynthia – F
Elijah – F
F. W. – F
Freeman W. – F
George – F
Georgie – F
Giles – N
Henry – J
John – D, F
John, Capt. – B
Lothrop – F
Lucy – F
Margaret – F
Mary – F
William – F
Zilpha – J

RIDER/RYDER
Abigail – K
Abner – N
Albertina T. – F
Amos, Capt. – F
Anna – F
Benjamin, Maj. – K
Betsey E. – F
Ebenezer, Jr. – N
Hannah – B
Job – D
John – F
Joseph – D, K
Joseph Jr. – D
Lucy Delano – D
Lydia – F
Mary – F

118

RIDER/RYDER
continued

Mehitable – F
Merrick – D
Patience – K
Rebecca – D
Samuel – F
Samuel, Captain – F
Sarah – N
Sarah E. – F
Seth – B
Southworth – D
Thomas – F
Tilden – K
William – F, K

RING
Eleazer – G
Susan – K
William – G

RIPLEY
Anna – C-W
Elizabeth – C-W
Levi – B
Leavitt – C-W
Nancy – C-W
Nancy Winslow – C-W
Nathaniel, Capt. – C-W
Nehemiah – C-E
Polly – B, C-W
William P. – C-W
William P., Dea – C-W
Wm. P. – C-W

ROBBINS/ROBINS
Adoniram D. – G
Albert R. – G
Alexander – F
Amasa – P
Ann Cushman – B
Ann G. Cushman – B
Ann S. – B
Ansel, Capt. – F
Betsey – B

ROBBINS/ROBINS
continued

Chandler – B
Chandler, Rev. – G
Charles , Capt., Master -
Mariner – B
Consider – F
Ebenezer – F
Edmund – F
Edward D. – G
Eleanor T. – P
Elizabeth – B
Eunice – F
Experience – B
Francis C. – P
Francis H. – C-E
Francis L. – P
Francis William – N
Frank C, - P
Frankie – P
George F – C-E
Hannah – F, G
Henry – N
Henry Augustus – N
Jane – G
Jesse – B, N
Joanna – F
John Briggs – C-E
Joseph – B
Josiah, Deacon – B
Josiah A. C-E
Josiah Adams – B
Josiah T, – B
Josiah Thomas – C-E
Josey – C-E
Julia Ann – F
L. T. – B
Leavitt T – B
Lemuel – B
Lemuel Cobb – F
Lemuel F. – B
Lemuel Stephen – B
Levi – F
Lewis F. – G
Lois – F

ROBBINS/ROBINS
continued

Lucia – B
Lucia R. – B
Lucia W. – B
Lydia – B
Lydia B. – B
Lydia F. – B
Margaret – B
Margaret H. – N
Margaret Lewis – N
Mary – B
Mary B. – B
Nathan B. – B
Nathan, Capt. – B
Nathaniel – F
Pamelia – G
Pella M. – B
Pella Morton – B
Rebecca J. – B
Rebecca Jackson – B
Rebecca W. C-E
Rev., Dr. – G
Rufus – F
Rufus, Capt. – B
Sally – B
Sally C. – G
Samuel, Jr. – G
Samuel, Capt. – G
Sarah – G
Sarah B. – B
Sarah J. P. – C-E
Sarah T. – N
Theophilus – F
Thomas C. – F
Thomas S. – P
Walter Jackson – C-E
William – F
William R. – B

ROBERTS
Eliza – C-E
Robert, Capt. – C-E
Sarah – C-E
Silvanus H. – C-E

119

ROBERTSON
David, Capt. – B
Mary – B

ROGERS
A. B. – N
Abigail – N
America – N
Betsey – F
Ellis – M
Eliza – N
Elizabeth – N
Elizebeth – N
Emma Frances – M
Ichabod – N
Irene Harlow – M
Jane – N
Jane F. – N
John – N
Lucretia – B
Lydia H. – C-E
Melinda – M
Nancy B. – N
Otis, Capt. – B
Polly – N
Rebecca – N
Samuel – N
Silvanus – N
William – N
William Jr. – N
William H. – N
Wm. – N

ROLFE
Horace H. – K
Mary Augusta – K
Mary T. – K

RUSSELL
Abigail – B
Betsey – B
Betsey F. – B
Betsey Farris – B
Bridgham – B
Brigham - B

RUSSELL continued
Charles – B
Elizabeth – B
James – B
James, Capt. – B
John – B
John, Capt. – N
Jonathan – B
Lucia – B
Mary – B
Mary Winslow – B
Mercy – B
Nancy – B
Rebecca – B
Thomas – B
Thomas, Hon. – B
William S. – B
Wm. S., Esq. – F

SALTONSTALL
Abigail – B
Richard, Hon., Esq. – B

SAMPSON
Abigail – K
Albert – L
Algemon Sidney – B
Alice B. – C-E
Alice Bradford – C-E
Caroline – B
Deborah – C-E
Elizabeth – C-E, N
George – B, K
Isaac – C-E, N
George Schuler – L
Hannah – B
Mary A. – C-E
Mary Allerton – C-E
Mary Ann – L
Milton – B
Patience – K
Phylander – G
Rebecca – C-E
Ruth – B
Ruth L. - B

SAMPSON
continued
Samuel – C-E
Sarah A. – G
Sarah E. – G
Sarah T. – L
Schulyer – L
Simeon, Capt. – C-E
Solomon – C-E
Stephen – K
Zabdiel, Esq. – B
Zabdiel, Hon. – B

SAMPSON
Benjamin – M
Deborah – C-E
Ebenezer – M
George – K
Hannah – M
Isaac – C-E
Jemima – G
Lazarus – G
Martha Washington C-E
Mary – C-E
Patience – K
Simeon – C-E
Simeon, Capt. – C-E

SAUNDERS
Betsey – B
John – B
Thomas S. – B

SAVERY
Abigail T. – B
Elizabeth – B
Lemuel – B
Louisa – F

SAWYER
Joshua – C-E

SCOTT
John Esq. – B
Phebe – B

120

SEARS
Bartlett, Capt. – B
Bathsheba – B
Belinda T. – E
Daniel H. – E
Eleazer – N
Eunice B. – N
Harriett N – N
Hiram R. – N
Mary Ann – N
Polly – N
Rebecah – N
Willard – N

SEARSON
Robert – L
Hannah – L
Sarah – L

SEYMOUR
Edward – B
Horace – B
Julia – B
Naomi – B

SHAW
Betsey – C-E
Betsey Holmes – C-E
Esther – C-E
Ichabod – C-E, C-W
Ichabod, Jr. – C-E
Lucia Russell – C-E
Maria – C-E
Mary – C-E
Mary S. – C-E
Mary Elizabeth – C-E
Mary Sampson – C-E
Priscilla – C-W
Rebecca Bartlett – C-E
Southworth – C-E
Wm. H. - M

SHERMAN
Cynthia T. – F
Elizabeth H. – N
Samuel – B
Sarah – G
William, Capt. – N

**SHURTLEFF/
SHURTLIFE**
Faith – B
Jabez, Capt. – B
James – B
Lydia – B
Mary – B
William, Capt. – B

SIMMONS
Abigail – A
Beulah – A
George, Capt. – A
Gershom – P
Iraetta – P
Joann White – A
Lemuel – A
Lorenzo – A
Lydia W. – P
Mercy – A
Moses – A
Priscilla – A

SMITH
Elizabeth – A
Henry – A
Mehitable P. – F
Phillip – A

SNOW
George F. – P
Leonard – P
Maria – P

SOMES
Lucia – B
Thomas – B

SOUTHWORTH
Edward – B
Jacob – B
Ruth B. - B

SPEAR
Clarrisa Harlow – C-E
Elizabeth R. – P
Ida Lizzie – P
Thomas – C-E

SPINKS
Nicholas – A
Sarah – A

SPINNEY
Abigail T. Savery – B
Robert Huntress – B
Thomas – B

SPOONER
Allen C. – P
Allen Crocker – P
Anna – P
Deborah – M
Ebenezer – J
Elizabeth – K
Ephraim – K
Fiona – P
Frona Elizabeth – P
James – P
Janis Walter – P
Lucy W. – P
Nathaniel – P
Sarah – J
Susan Harlow – P
Susan L. – P
Thomas – J
Tomb – A

STANDISH
Joshua – C-E
Lydia – C-E
Lydia Ann – C-E

STEPHENS

August Frances – C-E
Edward – B
Eleazer – B
Elisabeth – B
Elizabeth – B
Emma E. – C-E
Hannah – B
Jane – C-E
Mary – B
Mary D. – C-E
Nancy – B
Sarah – B
Susanna – B
William – B, C-E
William, Capt. – C-E
Wm. – B

STETSON

Abigail – B
Bradford – B
Caleb – B
Hervey – O
Mary – O

STEWARD

Bethiah – A
Claribel T. – A
George – P
Henry O. – A

STILLMAN

James E. – K

STRAFFIN

George – A
Mary S. – A
Robert – A

STURTEVANT

Elizabeth – A
Hannah – A, O, G
James – A
Jane – O
John – G

STURTEVANT

continued
Joseph – A
Joshua P. – A
Lucy – A, O
Marcia – A
Marcia Ann – A
Mercy – A
Mercy A. – A
Rebecca W. – O
Sally – O
Sarah – O
Sivanus – A
Thankfull – A
William – O
William, Capt. – O 43
William, Esq. – O
William W. – O
Zenas – A

SULLIVAN

James – L
Mary – P

SWAN

Charles S. – B
Charles T. – B
Hannah – B

SWIFT

Alice B. – L
Annabella – L
Deborah S. – L
Jabez – L
Jacob – L
Lucy B. – L
William – L

SWINBURN

Elon S. – L
Keziah D. – L
Robert – L

SYLVESTER

Abigail – B
Abner – B
Abner, Capt. – B
Elsey – B
M. B. – B
Mary Harlow – B
Nathaniel, Capt. – B
W. – B

SYMMES

Elizabeth – F
Hannah – K
Isaac – K
Joanna – K
Lazarus – F
Mary – F
Nancy H. – K
Polly – F

TALBOT

George W. – N
Jerusha – N
Jerusha T. – N
Nancy E. – N
Robert D. – N
Samuel – N

TAYLOR

Edward – B
Edward, Capt. – B
Jacob – F
Jacob, Capt. – F
James P. – L
Jemima – F
Mary – B
Nancy – L
Philip – L
Sarah – L
William – B

THACHER

Catherine – B
James – B
James, Dr. – B

THACHER continued
James Hersey B
Mary – B
Sukey – B
Susan – B
Susanna – B

THATCHER
Peter, Rev. Mr. – A

THOMAS
Benjamin – N
Daniel, Esq. – J
Deborah – M, N
Elizabeth – J
Hope – J
Jane – L
Joah – B
Job B. – F
John, Esq. – J
Joseph, Capt. – L
Josiah – N
Lois – B
Luce – J
Mary – J, L
Mercy – L
Nancy – L
Nathaniel – J, L
Nathaniel, Esq. – J
Nathaniel Hon Esq. – J, M
Nathanll – J
Priscilla – L
Tomb – A
William – J
William, MD – L
Wm. – L
Zeruah – B

THOMPSON/
THOMSON
Bella – A
Bethiah – A
Elizabeth – K
George D. – G
Irene – G

THOMPSON/
THOMSON continued
Julian – A
Louisa – K
Martin – A
Martin Benson – A
Seth – A
Zoraday – K

TILLEY
Elizabeth – H

TILLSON
Anna Hamblin – A
Edmond, Capt. – K
Edmund, Capt. – B
Elizabeth – B, K
Elizabeth – K
Hamblin – A, G
Maria – G
Perez – K
Susan B. – G
Susan Bradford – G
Susanna – A

TINKHAM
Jacob – B
Rebecca – B

TORREY
Betsey – M
Elizabeth – L, M
Heaviland – L
Heaviland, Dea – L
John – M
John, Col. – M
John, Dea – F
John, Esq. – M
Joseph – L
Joshua – N
Joshua, Dea – M
Mary – L, M
Meriah – M
Sally – N
William – L

TORSEY
Mary – F

TOTMAN
Isaac – J
Sarah – J
Simeon – J

TRASK
Jerusha – B
Joseph – B
Thomas – B
William – B

TRIBBEL/TRIBBLE
Albert – C-E
Alice B. – K
Augustus – B
Bathsheba – C-E
Betsey – B
Christiana D. – C-E
Cynthia T. – F
Desire C. – K
Francis – B
Gideon H. – B
Gustavus – C-E
Hiram – F
Horace G. – C-E
Isaac – B
J. – B
John – C-E
Joseph – A, B
Joseph Jr. – B
Lavantia – C-E
Lois – B
Marcia – C-E
Maria P. – F
Maria Thomas – F
Marston W. – C-E
Mary – B
Robert F. – B
Sarah – A, B
Thomas – F
Thomas, Capt. – F
William - B

123

TRIBBEL/TRIBBLE continued
William B. – K
William Thomas – F
Winslow – C-E
Wm. – B

TRIMBLE
Alice B. – K
Desire C. – K
William B. – K

TUFTS
Charles – G
Cordelia B. – G
Charles Henry – G
Elizabeth – M
Emma Cordelia – G
James W. – G
Jona – M
Jonathan – M
Mary Jane – G
Priscilla – M
Sarah – M
Sarah Elizabeth – G
William Drew – M

TURNER
David – B, D
Deborah – B
Eleazar – C-E
Elizabeth – B
Elizabeth H. – F
Jesse, Capt. – F
Jesse H. – F
Lothrop – B
Lothrop, Capt. – B
Lydia – B
Lydia Prince – B

Martha L. – D
Merca – B
Meroa – B
Patience – B
Patience C. – B
Patience Coleman – B

TURNER continued
Rebecca – B
Ruth – B
Ruth J. – D
Susan – B
Susanna – B

VAUGHAN
Oliver C. Capt. – C-E
Sarah H. – C-E

VIRGIN
Abigail – B
John, Capt. – B
Priscilla – B
William Henry – B

WADSWORTH
Charles – B
George E. – B
Susan E. – B

WAIT/WAITE
Elizabeth – B
Martha – B
Mary – B, L
Return – L
Richard – B

WARD
John – F

WARLAND
John – C-E
Sarah – C-E

WARREN
Abigail – K
Benjamin, Capt. – K, O
Benjamin, Maj. – O
Benjn, Maj. – B, O
C. J. – G
C. W. – G
David – O, P
David, Capt. – O

WARREN continued
Elizabeth – A, K
Esther – O
Gent. – A
George – P
Georgina Minerva – G
James – A
James, Col. Esq. – A
James, Esq. – A
James, Gen. – A
James, Esq., Hon – A
Jane – O
Josiah – A
Lois – O
Mary a. B. – P
Mercy – A
Na—n – A
Nathaniel – A
Patience – O
Penelope – A
Rebecca – B
Rebekah – B
Sally – O, P
Sally C. – P
Sarah – A
Tomb – A
William – K

WASHBURN
Bathsheba – L
Benjamin – L
Catherine – D
George – K
George, Capt. – K
Hannah J. – D
Isaac J. – D
John – L
Lydia – L
Margaret J. – K

Priscilla – G, K
Priscilla D. – K

WASHINGTON
Gen. - F

WATERMAN

Elka – O
Hannah – O
John – O
Six sons – O
Two dau. – O

WATSON

Abigail – B
B. M. – B
Benjamin – B
Benjamin M. Esq. – B
Benjamin Marston – B
Charles Lee – B
Daniel – B
Edward W. – B
Eliza Ann – B
Elizabeth – B
Elizabeth Miller – B
Elkanah – B
Eunice – B
George – B
George, Esq. – B
Harriet L. – M
John – B
John, Esq. – B
Jonathan Sturges – B
Lucia – B
Lucretia – B
Lucretia Ann – B
Lucretia Burr – B
Patience – B
Phebe, Madame – B
Priscilla – B
William – B
William, Esq. – B
William, Jr. – B
William, Hon – B
Winslow – M

WEBSTER

Ervin, Dr. – P
Harriet – P
Manly – P
Olin - P

WEST

Samuel – B

WESTGATE

Charles – K
Lydia – K
Lydia Ann – K

WESTON/ WESTRON

Ann M – K
Benjamin – K
Betsey – F
Clara – K
Coomer, Capt. – K
Elizabeth - F, K
Esther M. – G
George, Capt. – P
George Jr. – P
Hannah – K
Harriet – F
Harvey, Capt. – A, P
Hattie – K
Herbert L. – K
James H. – P
Jane Leonard – F
Joanna – K
Lewis – F, K
Lucy – A, K, P
Lydia – K
Lydia H. – P
Lydia M. – P
Mary – K, P
Mary Tilden – K
Nancy Carver - K
Oliver – F
Patty – K
Polly – P
Priscilla – B
Prudence – K
Rebecca – F
Sally C. – A
Sarah E. – A
Sarah Nye – K
Susan – F, K
Susan S. – K

**WESTON/
WESTRON
continued**

Seth – A
Thomas – K
William – K
William, Capt. – K
William L – K
Willie – K

**WETHEREIL/
WETHRELL/
WITHERELL/
WITHERLY**

Anna – D
Anna May – D
Elisabeth – D
Elizabeth – D
Hannah – B, D
Harriet – D
Isaac – D
Isaac, Rev. – D
John May – D
Joshua – D
Lemuel – D
Lemuell – D
Lucia – D
Nancy – D, F
Nancy Shaw – D
Rebecah – D
Rebeckah – D
Sarah – D
Thomas – D
Thomas Jr. – D
William – D

WHITE

Cornelius, Capt. – B
Elizabeth – B
Experience – B
Gideon, Capt. – B
Hannah – B
Joanna – B
Johanna – B
Thomas – B

125

WHITING
Arthur B. – D
Asa A. – K
Elizabeth – F
Ephraim – F
Joseph B. – D
Laura T. – D
Levi – N
Mary – N
Mary M. – K
Pelham – N
Priscilla – P
Sophia B. – N

WHITMARSH
Sarah – G

WHITTEN
Albertenia L. – F
Charles – C-W
Charles – F
Edward W. – F
Elijah C. – F
E. A. – F
Emeline A. – F
Harriet B. – B
Joseph W. – F
L. W. – F
Lewis H. – F
Lydia N. – C-W
Lydia M. C-W
Mary H. – C-W
Mary R. – F
Samuel – B
Samuel B. – B
Tenia – F
Willie Bradford – C-W

WILLIAMS
Elias – L
Eliza – A
Eliza Ann – A
John – A
Mary – L
Nancy – L

WINSLOW
Edward – B
Elizabeth – B

WITTE
Hans – L

WOOD
Betsey – C-W
Betsey S. – C-W
Eleanor – C-W
Elijah – C-W
Elijah, Jr. – C-W
Isaac – C-W
Perses – C-W
Pirses – C-W

WRIGHT
Elisabeth Abby – C-E
Elisabeth B. – C-E
Lorenzo – C-E
Joseph, Capt. – K
Otis – C-E
Sally – K
William – C-E

126

SOURCES:

Barbara J Bradford Robinson, Howard E Robinson. Cynthia L. Robinson: *Burial Hill in the 1990s, Plymouth, Massachusetts* A six year cemetery mapping project with descriptions, conditions and some photographs

Pilgrim Hall Museum, Plymouth, MA www.pilgrimhall.org/

Genealogy on line www.genealogy.com

John Alden websites www.alden.org

Robert S. Wakefield and Lydia Finlay, *Mayflower Families for Five Generations: James Chilton, Richard More, and Thomas Rogers*, volume 2 (Plymouth: General Society of Mayflower Descendants, 1974).

Donald F. Harris, "The More Children of the Mayflower: Their Shropshire Origins and The Reasons Why they were Sent Away," *Mayflower Descendant* 43:123-132, 44:11-20,109-118.

Sir Anthony Wagner, "The Origin of the Mayflower Children: Jasper, Richard and Ellen More", *New England Genealogical and Historical Register*, 114(1960):163.

Sir Anthony Wagner, "The Royal Descent of a Mayflower Passenger", *New England Genealogical and Historical Register* 124(1970):85-87.

William Bradford, *Of Plymouth Plantation*, ed. Samuel Morison (New York: Random House, 1952).

Eugene Aubrey Stratton, *Plymouth Colony: Its History and Its People, 1620-1691* (Ancestry Publishing: Salt Lake City, 1986).

Charles Edward Banks *"Planters of the Commonwealth"*

www.USHistory.org

A. S. Burbank: *Guide to Historic Plymouth*

Handbook of Old Burial Hill Plymouth, Massachusetts: Its History, Its Famous Dead, and Its Quaint Epitaphs -- Published by A. S. Burbank, Pilgrim Bookstore, Plymouth, Massachusetts -- Copyright, 1902 by A. S. Burbank, Plymouth, Massachusetts

Albert Christopher Addison, 1911: *The Plymouth Colony Archive Project*, The Romantic Story of the Mayflower Pilgrims

Photographs of Old Burial Hill headstones by T P Burbank

Made in the USA
Middletown, DE
04 September 2016